# BERLITZ®

# CORFU

**1988/1989 Edition**

D1024008

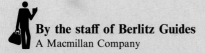

**By the staff of Berlitz Guides**
A Macmillan Company

# How to use our guide

- All the practical information, hints and tips that you will need before and during the trip start on page 97.

- For general background, see the sections The Island and the People, p. 6, and A Brief History, p. 13.

- All the sights to see are listed between pages 23 and 60, with suggestions for daytrips from Corfu described on pages 63 to 73. Our own choice of sights most highly recommended is pinpointed by the Berlitz traveller symbol.

- Entertainment, nightlife and all other leisure activities are described from pages 74 to 83 and 92 to 96, while information on restaurants and cuisine is to be found on pages 83 to 91.

- Finally, there is an index at the back of the book, pp. 126–128.

---

*Although we make every effort to ensure the accuracy of all the information in this book, changes occur incessantly. We cannot therefore take responsibility for facts, prices, addresses and circumstances in general that are constantly subject to alteration. Our guides are updated on a regular basis as we reprint, and we are always grateful to readers who let us know of any errors, changes or serious omissions they come across.*

---

Text: Don Larrimore
Photography: Daniel Vittet
Layout: Doris Haldemann
We're particularly grateful to Mike Mikeletis and Vicky Nicolopoulou for their help in the preparation of this book. We also wish to thank the Greek National Tourist Organization for its valuable assistance.
Cartography: ✦ Falk-Verlag, Hamburg.

**4**

# Contents

**Maps**

*Cover picture:* islet of Vlachérna

5

# This is Corfu

## The Island and the People

It really *is* an emerald isle on a turquoise sea. And happily the beauty of Corfu which has enchanted visitors through the centuries has survived the mounting incursions of the modern world. Inviting places to get away from it all are scattered liberally along the island's coastline and throughout the hilly hinterland.

Although indisputably Greek, Corfu is not typically Hellenic. In atmosphere as well as geography, it's more western than any other part of Greece. Almost 500 years of Venetian, French and British occupation left its mark here, but the Turks—who conquered the rest of Greece—failed to make a lasting impression. Since union with the mainland more than a century ago, Corfu has proudly styled itself Greece's western gateway, its entry to the Adriatic.

The island's shape resembles a scythe—in Greek *drépanon,* which was one ancient name for Corfu. Geologists say it's the exposed crown of a submerged mountain range

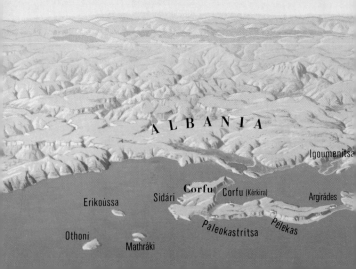

that broke off from the Greek-Albanian mainland back in the recesses of time. As the crow flies (but certainly not as the road runs), the island is about 40 miles long, north to south, while its width ranges from 2½ to 18 miles.

This greenest of Greece's 1,425 proper islands is arguably the prettiest as well. You can't blame Homer *(The Odyssey)* and Shakespeare *(The Tempest)* for choosing Corfu as literary settings—if indeed they did. Trees, flowering bushes and shrubs cloak practically all of its rolling landscape. Even tourists with little scientific interest in nature find themselves wondering about the name of a butterfly or the age of an olive tree.

What many visitors remember most about Corfu are the pellucid blue-greens of the Ionian and the endless groves of silvery olive trees. The sea itself is extraordinary; in any cove, the range of blues seems to defy the colour spectrum. And the water is usually so clear fish can't hide from view.

Ashore, on undulating hills and stone-hedged terraces, stand Corfu's incomparable olive trees, between 3 and 4 million of them. Their multiple trunks knotted and gnarled, these prized trees, of-

GREECE

ávos          Paxí          Antípaxi

Lefkás

IONIAN SEA

F. Hob/a/l

ten more than 500 years old, still provide excellent olive oil. But Corfu is also graced with legions of lemon and orange trees that exude a glorious aroma, with plane trees, acacia, myrtle, wisteria, oleander and grape arbours; with huge clusters of roses and vibrantly coloured wild flowers.

There's a reason for Corfu's

remarkably luxuriant vegetation: more rain falls here—trapped by the nearby mainland mountains—than over most of Greece. But don't despair. For the greater part of the year, this is very much an island in the sun.

When it comes to beaches, Corfu takes top honours. There are variations to meet all tastes: strips of pure sand, pebble or shingle alone or mixed with sand, with a gradual or immediate drop to

*Corfiotes from all walks of life make music; some crow about it.*

swimming depth for waders or plungers, and rocks for diving. Swells for surfing can be found on the western shores and calm bays for children on the protected east coast.

The sound of the sea slapping the shore, the twittering of a thousand birds, the braying of donkeys, the odd-hour crowing of cocks—these are the musical motifs of Corfu. Adding to the medley, you'll almost always hear the strains of Greek traditional music and, inevitably, the transistorized sounds of today's younger generation. One of the Corfiotes' fondest pastimes is singing: children and elders, in groups or on their own, sing happily and unselfconsciously.

About 92,000 people live on this idyllic isle. Many of them have never left it. Instead, the outside world comes to them—recently in sharply increasing numbers. Yet the natives will tell you that when the first plane landed on Corfu, not so very long ago, people stared admiringly into the sky and exclaimed, "Look at that bird; it must be 300 years old!"

Naturalness, lack of artifice, is one of the most endearing qualities of these islanders. Though reputed to be rather more sophisticated than many of their compatriots, the people of Corfu retain a fresh, open simplicity. Their legendary friendliness might date back to Homeric forebears: visitors today, even in tour groups, are made to feel just as welcome here as Ulysses was by the king of the Phaeacians and his beauteous daughter.

Being interested in their visitors, Corfiotes are likely to ask a lot of questions—often things that would be considered too "personal" elsewhere. Few secrets survive on this island where most doors remain unlocked. Crime is extremely rare, violent crime unheard of.

Corfiotes have their full measure of Greek *filótimo,* a quiet dignity and pride noticeable at all levels of society. There's a bit of the philosopher in every Greek.

To an outsider, Corfiotes can seem elaborately casual, their pace of life unhurried—if not downright disorganized. "We are a calm people", they say. Visitors accustomed to speed and efficiency often find this maddening. But impatience also exists. The characteristically Greek lack of discipline is very evident at bus stops, shop counters and bank tellers' windows, where only **9** foreigners would dream of queuing up docilely.

Home is where every Corfiote's heart really lies. Family life tends to be very close and affectionate with an immense amount of attention lavished on small children. And people take the Orthodox religion, with its elaborate ceremonies, most seriously here. Black-robed priests, their beards often white, are a common sight all round the island.

Language is no problem for most island visitors. A surprisingly large number of Corfiotes speak English or Italian, and most important signs are printed in both Greek and Latin alphabets.

One little-advertised feature of Corfu is a glimpse at Europe's most remote and isolated country—Albania. The towering mountains and sparsely inhabited coastline of this forbidden land lie tantalizingly near (a mile and a half from Corfu's north-eastern

coast), yet light-years away.

Perhaps the most marvellous thing about Corfu is that it has absorbed so much yet changed so little. Peasant women still jog along side-saddle on their mules carrying home bundles of firewood, scarcely glancing up at the giant jetliners zooming in for a landing.

Bikinis do not yet outnumber the traditional triple-layered dresses of older Corfiote women. Sleek sports cars roar off the ferries from Italy—and quickly slow to a frustrating crawl behind 19th-century horse carriages.

There are a few disturbing signs of "progress"—concrete constructions that mar certain

*A local beauty shows off her traditional costume; right: after the fishing boats come home, their nets are unfurled in the harbour.*

coastlines and soaring, big-city prices for shellfish.

But, gazing at the fishing nets hanging in the sunset as they always have, one some- how feels that the beauty of this emerald isle will endure, as Corfu itself has, despite all manner of assault over the past 2,500 years.

## It's Greek to Me

Finding your way around in Corfu is facilitated by the local practice of subtitling many Greek road signs with a version in the Latin alphabet, the form generally adopted in this guide. But watch out: the Greeks themselves don't always agree, and you will come across various spellings of the same word. For instance, *ágios* (saint) may also be seen written as *ághios* or *áyios*.

In the case of well-known sites (like Athens and Corfu) and proper names in a historical or literary context, we've used the time-honoured English spelling.

Stress, a very important feature of the Greek language, is indicated by an accent mark (′) over the vowel of the syllable to be emphasized.

Two words you'll want to learn immediately are ΠΛΑΤΕΙΑ *(platía)*, meaning square, and ΟΔΟΣ *(odós)*, street, which is often omitted in addresses.

For more about modern Greek spelling and pronunciation, see ALPHABET in the Blueprint section of this book.

# A Brief History

Shipwrecked on his way home from the Trojan War, Ulysses was washed ashore on the island of Scheria, exhausted and unclothed. Princess Nausicaa found him, Homer relates, and her father, King Alcinous of the mythical, seafaring Phaeacians, provided a boat to take the hero back to his native Ithaca.

That final stop-over on Ulysses' hazardous ten-year odyssey took place on what is now generally, if romantically, assumed to be Corfu. Try as they may, archaeologists have unearthed absolutely no proof linking this much-loved legend to the island.

Corfu's acknowledged history begins in 734 B.C., when the Corinthians established a colony called Corcyra here and drove away Liburnian pirates. Prospering from trade with southern Italy, Corcyra soon set up her own colonies on the nearby mainland and developed into an unexpectedly strong maritime power. In 665 B.C., she defeated Corinth in what Thucydides records as the first naval battle in Greek history, thus gaining her independence.

In the 25 centuries since that time, Corfu has suffered bom- **13**

*Though still somewhat fearsome, the monumental Gorgon pediment is now more than 2,500 years old and will not turn you to stone.*

bardment, assault, pillage, revolution and often terribly destructive occupation. For this strategically located island, with its safe harbours and fertile soil, was always an enticing prize worth fighting over by the myriad powers who contested control of the Adriatic and Ionian seas.

Calling on Athens for help in another maritime clash with Corinth in 433 B.C., little Corfu was largely responsible for setting off the Peloponnesian War. While the Greek world suffered 30 years of devastation in that struggle between Athens and Sparta, civil wars raged on nearly forgotten Corfu.

## A Roman Conquest

Gravely weakened, the island then fell prey to attacks by Spartans, Illyrian pirates and other enemies. A Roman fleet arrived and took control of Corfu before 200 B.C., making the empire's first conquest across the Adriatic.

Rome held nominal sway for five and a half centuries. En route to and from battles, or simply as tourists, Nero, Tiberius, Cato, Cicero, Caesar, Octavian and Antony (with Cleopatra) were among the Roman notables who visited Corfu. St. Jason and St. Sosipatros brought Christianity to the island before A.D. 200.

When the Roman empire split in the 4th century, the eastern section, Byzantium, took Corfu over administratively but didn't provide much security. Rampaging Vandals raided Corfu in 445. Even worse was the invasion in 562 by a horde of Ostrogoths who, true to form, savagely destroyed the island's ancient capital and most of its monuments.

After foiling an attempted takeover by Slavs in 933, the Corfiotes built their first fortress on the rocky bluff commanding the town's eastern sea approach; the citadel still stands.

Then came a notable new enemy: several times between 1080 and 1185, Norman forces crossed the Ionian from Sicily to seize Corfu and nearby island outposts of the enfeebled Byzantine empire. In desperation, Constantinople called on the Venetians for help. They responded and thereafter took an active interest in the destiny of the Adriatic gateway island.

When Doge Enrico Dandolo and the crusaders conquered Constantinople in 1204, Venice's spoils included western Greece, the Peloponnesus and all the Ionian islands. Since that was too much for the small if powerful maritime republic to handle, Venice left Corfu to a series of mostly peaceable medieval occupying forces for almost 200 years—naturally retaining commercial concessions.

For half of the 13th century, when ruled by the despots of Epirus, the island was administratively linked to the Greek mainland. The ruins of their hilltop castle of San Angelo remain today high above Paleokastrítsa on Corfu's west coast.

In 1259, Corfu was given to King Manfred, the Hohenstaufen King of Sicily, by Michael II of Epirus as his daughter's dowry. That situation lasted only eight years until Charles d'Anjou, the new King of Sicily and Naples, assumed control of the island; it remained under the Anjou family (Angevins) for more than a century. During that time Roman Catholicism, officially practised, almost snuffed out Corfu's traditional Eastern Orthodoxy.

**Venetian Rule**

When the Angevin dynasty came to an end, Corfu's fledgling assembly of 24 barons invited Venice to send in a protective military force. As always, marauding corsairs presented a danger. The Vene- **15** tians landed on June 3, 1386, beginning an occupation that was to continue without interruption for more than four centuries.

Corfu quickly became a key restocking port for the Serene Republic's galleys plying far-flung trading routes. To strengthen the defences of its vital harbour, the Venetians turned Corfu Town's old Byzantine fort into an effectively impregnable bastion. It was a wise move. And it changed the island's fate.

In 1463, after sweeping through mainland Greece, the Ottoman empire declared war on Venice. The Turks mounted assaults over succeeding years on the Ionian islands of Zakynthos (Zante), Cephalonia, Ithaca and Levkas. In 1537 it was Corfu's turn.

To punish Venice for putting galleys in its way as it sailed through the narrow Corfu channel, an Ottoman fleet landed troops and cannons intending to conquer the citadel. The bitter attack on the fortress (renowned in Corfiote history) failed, but the rest of the island was brutally plundered and the vengeful Turks carried off 15,000 prisoners—nearly half of Corfu's population. One captive, a particularly comely Corfiote,

later became the wife of a Turkish sultan. Practically all the other prisoners were bound into slavery.

Because the great siege had come from the capital's northwest, the Venetians erected a "new fort" (still called that today) to guard that approach and greatly strengthened other fortifications around the town.

In 1571, Corfu sent 1,500 seamen to toil on Venetian galleys engaged in the famous naval battle of Lepanto in the gulf of Patras, thus helping the Holy League of Christians defeat the Moslem Turks. This last major confrontation of oared ships marked the island's first naval triumph in many centuries. Nonetheless, it was a mere pinprick for the Ottoman empire, whose might continued to grow.

In 1716 came Corfu's finest military hour, again against the Turks and again at great cost. After losing the Peloponnesus and Athens to Venetian forces, the Ottoman sultan successfully counter-attacked and retook some of the Ionian islands. Then he sent 30,000 troops to quell Corfu.

Venice had hired foreign regiments under German mercenary commander Johann Matthias von der Schulenburg to defend the island. For six bloody weeks they held out in Corfu Town. The Turks, with their overwhelmingly superior forces, ravaged the rest of the island and seemed about to capture the capital.

But, suddenly, the Turks called off their assault and sailed away. Perhaps they were frightened by one of those legendarily ferocious Corfu thunder and hail storms, or perhaps—as the populace devoutly believes—the island's patron saint, Spirídon, intervened.

In any case, they didn't return to try again. Thus Corfu is the only part of Greece never subjugated by the Ottomans. A statue of Schulenburg was quickly erected. It stands proudly today outside the entrance to the Old Fort.

Throughout its long feudal occupation, Venice kept Corfu firmly in tow, a colony valued but not rewarded as an important naval base, trading depot, customs-collection station and supply centre. A civil-military governor and some

*Its guns long silent, this durable fort recalls Corfu's heroic times.*

senior bureaucrats dispatched from Venice ran the island. Co-operative Corfiote nobles held lesser administrative posts and flowery titles, but

*Splendid silver coffin holds relics of island's beloved St. Spiridon.*

ordinary islanders fared badly.

Corfu was allowed no public education during these four centuries; nothing was done to restore the Greek Orthodox religion to its traditional dominance among the doggedly faithful people; and Italian replaced Greek as the official

## St. Spirídon

Corfiotes swear by him, pray to him, name their sons after him and honour him with truly remarkable passion. He's the island's universally loved patron saint, yet he wasn't even born here!

A village shepherd on the distant island of Cyprus, Spirídon became a monk, then a bishop noted for devoutness and the ability to effect minor miracles. When he died in A.D. 350, his remains were taken to Constantinople. But just before the Turkish occupation in the 15th century, they were smuggled out in a sack of straw strapped to a mule. Spirídon arrived on Corfu in 1460 and in time became the object of enthusiastic veneration.

Colourful processions are staged in Corfu Town on Orthodox Palm Sunday and Easter Saturday, August 11 and the first Sunday in November to commemorate Spirídon's major miracles. He reputedly saved the island on four occasions: twice from the plague, once from famine and once (1716) from the Turks.

Small wonder that most Corfu men are named Spíros.

language, although the peasants couldn't understand it and had no way of learning it. Many Corfiotes laboured as serfs in the Venetian aristocratic villas which still dot the countryside.

More happily, Venice was responsible for most of the olive trees that grace Corfu's landscape: anxious to ensure a constant supply of oil, the republic at one stage decreed a cash bonus for every 100 trees planted in the Ionian islands. Perhaps the most visible legacy is Corfu's old city: with its narrow streets and high buildings, it's the most Venetian town in Greece.

## Bonaparte's Dream Island

In 1797, the republic of the doges fell to Napoleon, thus ending 411 years of Venetian occupation of Corfu. For reasons which remain obscure, Napoleon was rather obsessed with the island. "The greatest misfortune which could befall me is the loss of Corfu", he wrote to his foreign minister, Talleyrand. So immediately after capturing Venice, Napo- **19** leon sent a force to occupy Corfu and the other Ionian islands, which soon passed legally to France under the Treaty of Campo Formio.

The French occupiers replaced Venice's autocratic government with democratic representation, burned the "Golden Book" of nobility at Corfu Town, introduced public education and made Greek the official language. But, nonetheless, they antagonized the islanders by continuing the suppression of the Orthodox Church. After less than two years, the Bonapartists were driven out of Corfu by a joint Russian-Turkish force that reinstated Greek Orthodoxy as the official religion.

Eight years later, in 1807, France regained Corfu from the Russians by the Treaty of Tilsit. Napoleon, who never actually had a chance to visit what he called "the key to the Adriatic", garrisoned the citadels with 50,000 men equipped with 500 new cannons, making it the most powerful fortified point in the eastern Mediterranean area, according to Corfiote historians.

In the last seven Napoleonic years, the French established the first Ionian academy for the promotion of arts and sciences, imported printing presses that turned out periodicals, drew up a street plan for Corfu Town, built a miniature Rue de Rivoli (the Listón) and introduced cultivation of the potato and tomato to wary islanders.

During this time, the British carried on an ineffectual but irritating blockade of the island. In 1809, they captured four other Ionian islands from the French but couldn't hope to conquer heavily defended Corfu.

## The British Move In

Napoleon's luck finally ran out. After his defeat at the battle of Leipzig in 1813, the British took over Corfu. The following year, the Treaty of Paris made the seven Ionian islands—Corfu, Paxos, Levkas, Ithaca, Cephalonia, Zante and Kithera—an independent "state" under the protection of Britain. Corfu was the capital, Sir Thomas Maitland the first lord high commissioner.

The British occupation of Corfu lasted half a century. While controversial, this protectorate brought certain benefits: the best road network on any Greek island, a water-supply system that still operates in Corfu Town, a decent judiciary, hospitals, model prisons, the island's first university and religious freedom ensuring the primacy and independence of the Orthodox Church.

Maitland's constitution (1817) was another matter. Though presenting the façade of parliamentary government with a Corfiote senate and assembly, the high commissioner actually retained all the power. Some of the measures introduced on the island were pure personal caprice on the part of the ten English high commissioners.

The first serious unrest under the British occurred in the 1820s. Mainland Greece was engaged in the struggle against Turkey, but Maitland stopped the Corfiotes from giving any assistance to their Greek compatriots. Understandably, this engendered popular bitterness.

After Greece had become independent and sentiment for union with the mainland was rising, the British introduced token constitutional reforms, freeing the press and liberalizing election procedures. But the high commissioner's power remained intact. Nationalistic agitation for union— *énosis*—continued to grow until even the most stubborn colonialist on Corfu could see the writing on the wall.

## Greek at Last

In 1863, when the pro-British Prince William of Denmark became King George I in Athens, Corfu and the other six Ionian islands were ceded to Greece. A big-power agreement declared the islands "perpetually neutral", and the British blew up the powerful fortifications they had added to Corfu Town before hauling down the Union Jack. When they sailed off, Corfu's assembly declared its gratitude to Queen Victoria for this unprecedented voluntary withdrawal by a great power from an overseas possession.

The British left behind a number of stately buildings and monuments. Cricket, ginger beer and Christmas chutney remain Corfu favourites today.

Tranquillity and flocks of aristocratic tourists descended on Corfu in its early years as a province of Greece. Empress Elisabeth of Austria liked the island so much that she commissioned a startlingly elaborate palace south of Corfu Town (see p. 56).

During World War I, Corfu served as an Allied military **21**

*The island's venerable olive trees shade grazing sheep from hot sun.*

and naval base, echoing the role the island had played in centuries past. In 1923, Mussolini ordered his fleet to bombard Corfu in reprisal for the alleged assassination of an Italian general on the Greek-Albanian border. Italian forces briefly occupied the island until obliged to withdraw under diplomatic pressure (primarily from Great Britain). The Italians returned as occupiers in World War II. Mussolini issued new currency and renamed streets, signalling his intention to annex the Ionian islands. But in 1943 Italy capitulated.

When the Germans tried to succeed their defeated allies, the Italian troops resisted on both Corfu and its sister island of Paxos. In the ensuing battle, about one-quarter of Corfu

# Where to Go

For visitors who come to Corfu mainly to relax in the sun, there's good news: the island has practically no "must" sightseeing. In most un-Greek fashion, they haven't even unearthed a significant archaeological site! But be advised: topography conspires against those who would "do" Corfu in two or three days. The best beaches, prettiest panoramic vistas and most charming rural areas are scattered, and two-thirds of the coastline has neither a road nor a path.

Nonetheless, this is a small island, so no matter where you're staying, alluring locations are close by. Tour groups and travel agencies offer bus or caïque excursions with principal sights with English-speaking guides, but many wonderful spots are overlooked.

Much the best way to enjoy the island is to meander at will by car or boat. Bring your own car, if you can: renting one for a day can easily cost as much as your hotel room.

A tremendously popular Corfu solution is to hire a motorscooter or bicycle for short ventures. Young people and others with time to spare

Town was destroyed, including the Ionian parliament house, the academy and the municipal theatre. After a year of occupation, German forces were evacuated in October 1944. The British moved in right behind them, and peace finally descended again.

Despite civil upheavals since the war, tourism and agriculture—Corfu's two economic mainstays—have now brought unprecedented prosperity to much of the island.

23

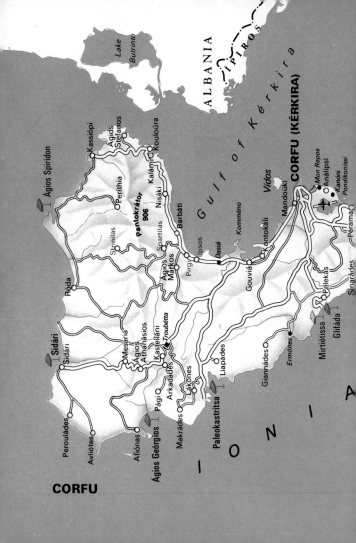

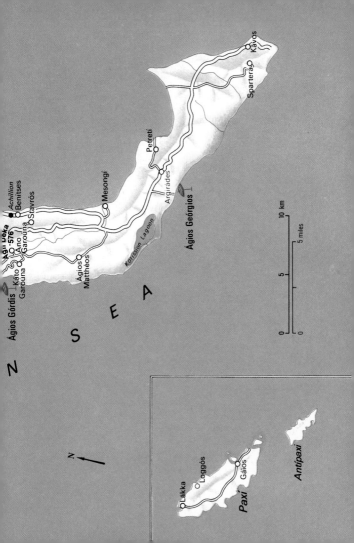

often hitchhike. It's legal, safe, and usually successful.

Most Corfiotes get around the island by bus, which is cheap if not always un-crowded. Buses take you to within striking distance of many remote and lovely places, though getting back on the infrequent services may be a problem.

Finally, for nature lovers nothing can beat walking through Corfu's ever-inviting countryside.

The normal way to begin a book on Corfu would be with its capital, Corfu Town. But the island's compelling attractions lie elsewhere—in its bountiful natural assets, its splendid beaches, charming coves, rolling hills and silvery olive groves. This is what Corfu is all about.

*Just one of six blue-green coves to be explored at Paleokastritsa.*

# Paleokastrítsa

Once you see it, you may well join the legions of travellers who fondly proclaim this the loveliest scenery in the entire Mediterranean. Paleokastrítsa offers something special for swimmers, snorkellers, sailors or strollers.

Six small coves with incredibly turquoise water nestle in a coastline of hills and promontories draped in olive, cypress and lemon trees. Strips of

partly sandy, partly shingle beach ring the shoreline; sea grottoes yawning out of sheer cliffs invite exploration.

Perched on the main, pleasantly wooded promontory glistens a neat Byzantine monastery; you will often see the handful of priests leading their small flock of sheep back and forth to pasture.

It's assumed locally that Paleokastrítsa was the site of King Alcinous's fabulous palace (see p. 13). Though archaeologists haven't produced even a shard of ancient pottery to support this notion, the magnificent setting is certainly worthy of Homer's effusive prose.

Offshore from Paleokastrítsa a large, graceful rock called **Kolóvri** stands erectly against the Ionian surf. An endearing Corfu legend asserts that this rock was Ulysses' ship. Poseidon, it's said, was so angry when he learned the Phaeacians of Scheria had provided Ulysses with transport that he petrified their vessel on the return voyage. Even skeptics concede that Kolóvri *does* resemble a ship. Oblivious to the rock's mythological significance, sea birds now lay their eggs on it, in nests sheltered by a sturdy cactuslike plant called *frangosikiá*. **27**

The fine 25-kilometre road from Corfu Town to Paleokastrítsa on the north-west coast has been the best road on the island since its construction 150 years ago by British engineering troops. And therein lies a Corfiote tale: while the official reason for the road was to link the British garrison to a military convalescent camp at Paleokastrítsa, it's said that Sir Frederick Adam, the high commissioner, really had the road built so he and his Corfiote wife could easily reach their favourite picnic spot.

Despite its fame, Paleokastrítsa had until recently escaped any tampering with its natural beauty. The year-round population is less than three dozen, but this is hard to believe during the high season when several hundred Corfiotes move down from their nearby hillside homes to serve the hordes of visitors who jam Paleokastrítsa's hotels and villas.

Most of the construction is new, and not all of it is praiseworthy. But no building has been permitted to crowd the 16th-century **monastery** that stands at the end of the Adam road.

"Please do not enter the monastery in bathing suits or shorts", reads a sign at the entrance. Inside the gleaming, whitewashed walls, visitors may be offered a glass of refreshingly cold water by a monk at the old-fashioned well. Past lemon trees and carefully tended flower gardens is a pretty chapel. A one-room museum has some fantastic shells and huge bones, probably whale, extracted from the sea early last century, as well as icons several centuries old, and mustily venerable religious books. (One icon was stolen recently by a thief who substituted a poor copy: a sensationally rare case of crime for Corfu.) Though the items in an adjacent souvenir shop are decidedly not Byzantine, the atmosphere elsewhere around this spotless monastery is. Unfortunately, monasteries on Corfu no longer offer rooms to visitors.

Outside the main gate past the unmenacing cannon, wander up beyond the monks' vegetable gardens and tiny cemetery until you reach the clifftop lookouts with breathtaking views of the sea and rocks far below.

Paleokastrítsa has the repu-

*Time seems to stand still inside the serene 16th-century monastery.*

tation of being one of the best places in Greece for fresh lobster. Actually, the lively creatures displayed by the seaside restaurants here are more often saltwater crayfish (see p. 86), but if you can afford them, they're delicious.

During the season, Paleokastrítsa is best in the early morning and early evening when the crowds and the jarring sounds of auto and scooter motors give way to the chirping of birds and the gentle whoosh of surf on shore.

At any time of the year or day, the finest view of Paleokastrítsa is from a lookout point high above the coastline. Only the hardiest attempt the 1,000-foot climb from sea level, but happily there's no need: a narrow, asphalted road twists up 4 kilometres through olive groves to the precariously perched village of LÁKONES*. A short way on, at a café called with great understatement "Bella Vista", is a magnificent **panorama**, one of the finest in Europe.

All of Paleokastrítsa, the spectacular shoreline and even Corfu Town itself (25 km. away) are visible. Paleo-

kastrítsa's coves fan out below: from left to right, AGÍA TRIÁS, PLATÁKIA, ALÍPA, ÁGIOS SPIRÍDON, ÁGIOS PÉTROS and ABELÁKI. The first three cluster together like clover leaves, forming a larger bay.

Looking down, you see the monastery jutting dramatically over azure water—a superb location. If King Alcinous didn't put his palace there 3,000 years ago, he should have.

---

* Every second spring, after the olive harvest, visitors can linger to watch the village's three olive presses in action.

Whether or not Ulysses was a visitor, local people have no doubts about more recent celebrities. Kaiser Wilhelm made a big impression when he turned up at Paleokastrítsa early this century. He was the first to arrive by motor-car, and it's still recalled how everyone thought he must be the devil incarnate in that infernal machine. Yugoslav President Tito came by yacht, as did the Onassises and a collection of film stars.

Just below Paleokastrítsa is the large, attractive bay of LIAPÁDES, your first glimpse of the sea when arriving by road. Though it's best explored by boat, simple tracks lead to the partly sandy, summarily developed GÉFIRA beach, where you can swim in what Corfiotes call their "green waters". The setting of

*Engaging friendliness and simplicity greet you in Corfu's villages.*

cypress trees is glorious. Four other little coves tucked into the bay's rocky shoreline offer seclusion to those who prefer the undressy style of sunbathing.

Beyond Liapádes Bay are two absolutely unspoiled pebbly and sandy beach strips. Named **Homoús** and **Stiliári**, they run beneath huge cliffs which bear amazingly symmetrical scars from millions of years of waves and wind. As your boatman will point out, there's no possible way to get here except by sea—certainly not by foot over those severe cliffs, nor even by helicopter.

The crystal-clear sea is full of fish and underwater scenery for snorkellers. Looming at you here from just a mile offshore is Kolóvri, which, even so close, seems as if it just might be Ulysses' petrified ship...

## A Tale of 6½ Beaches

You can swim along most of Corfu's 117 nautical miles of coastline. But the island has few truly excellent *sand* beaches, and none at all on the eastern shore where most hotels are located. Shingle, or pebble, and rocky bathing areas abound—many of them very attractive. If you're will-

ing to make the effort to get to them, Corfu has 6½ outstanding, golden sand beaches—often quite out of the way.

**Mirtiótissa,** across the island from Corfu Town, is claimed by some enthusiasts to be the most beautiful beach in Europe. Sheer cliffs covered with trees and shrubs drop directly to the sand, creating a sense of isolation enhanced by the absence of man-made structures. From the surrounding greenery comes the chirping of hundreds of birds.

This open Ionian side of Corfu almost always has some surf; but in summer it's usually gentle because the sandy bottom descends very gradually to swimmable depth. At both ends of the long beach curl rocky promontories offering marvellous snorkelling in crystal-blue water.

This enchanting beach completely vanishes from time to time. During the winter, when high Ionian waves pound the shore and torrents of fresh rain water plummet from the cliffs, the sand is carried out to

sea. Inevitably it comes back again with milder tides.

Maps seem deliberately vague, and, as yet, no sign advertises Mirtiótissa. It's half an hour by foot from the nearest bus stop on the Pélekas—Vátos road, and, for car or scooter travellers, a bumpy ride along the dirt track which winds through the olive groves. If you are lucky, peasants will direct you—otherwise right at the first fork, left at the second and right at the third brings you to the glistening sands.

The beach's solitude is not all it was, what with eating places nearby, but its natural grandeur remains unspoiled.

*Hilly coves of Paleokastrítsa seen from above; right: Orthodox tradition shared with a new generation.*

**33**

It has become Corfu's un-officially recognized "nudist" beach, and there are informal sports competitions organized.

Follow a footpath at the northern end of the beach up through the trees to the small, whitewashed **monastery of Mirtiótissa** (Our Lady of the Myrtles). It's built on a superb site where, the story goes, a monk found an icon of the Virgin Mary in a myrtle bush.

The other way to reach this beach is by boat. This enchanting trip can be arranged from Paleokastrítsa, Ermónes or Glifáda.

To the south of Mirtiótissa, the wide sprawling beach of **Glifáda** has lately experienced the mixed blessings of civilization. The new asphalt road, tracing hairpin curves down over the coastal hills to shore level, brings vehicles full of sand-and-surf seekers. Despite being so large, the beach does become crowded in high season.

Parents with small children particularly appreciate Glifáda's shallow water and tiny wavelets. Serious swimmers

*Mirtiótissa, an enchanted spot where you feel miles away from it all; right: seaside artistry.*

must go out a bit to reach deep water.

Glifáda (about 16 km. across the island from Corfu Town) is a relatively easy car, bus or taxi ride from most of the island's hotels. The long, sandy beach is dominated by a grand hotel. The swimming is superb; sailing boats and

Corfu's west coast has two widely separated beaches called St. George *(Ágios Geórgios)*, both long and minimally developed. For identification purposes they may be designated *bay* and *beach*. The trip to **St. George's Bay,** in the north, is memorable, whether you travel by road or by

pedalos are available. Enough *tavérnes* and discos for all.

The normal route to Glifáda climbs through the charming hill village of PÉLEKAS, noted for the "Kaiser's Throne". The German emperor used to motor to this lookout point above the village to watch the sunsets.

motorboat from Paleokastrítsa.

Once over the beautiful TROUBÉTTA pass with its vistas of Corfu's mountainous north, the drive is pure pleasure—particularly between the villages of ARKADÁDES and PÁGI. You wind past lush gorges with springtime water- **35** falls, through timeless groves of olives and clusters of cypress, slowing down every now and then for sheep, goats and mules in the road.

Tourism has barely made its mark here in the north-west. The old peasant women in their blue-and-white costumes will still gaze curiously at you and then wave. Shepherds as wizened as olive trunks will shake their staffs in greeting. Down the final four kilometres from sleepy Pági to the beach, the curves and ruts in the surface are more friendly than menacing.

Compellingly beautiful, too, is the half-hour boat trip from Paleokastrítsa to St. George's Bay. You chug along past jagged cliffs which dwarf your bobbing outboard, peeking into mysterious sea caves and keeping a watch for dolphins that often cavort in these waters. Rounding the edge of the bay, you're likely to come upon a fishing boat or two working nets. The area is known for rewarding catches, so you'll probably find the freshest possible fish at the modest eating places here.

But these little restaurants are only incidental interruptions along the wide, solitary, windswept beach, which **36** forms a leisurely arc some 2

miles long. Once you settle down on this vast expanse of sand to watch a seagull circling overhead, civilization seems very far away.

In fact, Corfu Town is less than 32 kilometres away. A useful, though infrequent, bus service goes to AFIÓNAS, still a good walk away down a dirt track to the beach.

The long, desolate strip known as **St. George's Beach** is southern Corfu's only superior sandy shore. Though limited accommodation is available, the coast seems likely to remain unspoiled for some time to come. While only about 35 kilometres from Cor-

fu Town, group tours rarely visit it, and the public bus stops a 15-minute walk away.

Here you can wander for miles, idly examining whatever the sea has washed up. Bathers are relatively few—even though a tarred road leads directly to the beach.

The beach has several simple café-restaurants and some inoffensive beach bungalows and villas. Unpaved tracks run along the shoreline in both directions from the paved road and then peter out. To the north as far as the KORIS-SÍON lagoon the coast features sand dunes. This virgin area—no roads, no buildings, no drinking water—is perfect for swimming and sunning, and in fact its relatively slow development is due to the lack of trees and shade.

Heading left (south) along the shoreline from the paved road, you'll come upon a bluff sheltering marvellous coves with yellow-brown sand. This is still within reasonable walking distance of the little bit of "civilization" near the crossroads.

Much closer to the capital

*It's well worth the effort to get to fine sandy beach of St. George.*

*Some delightfully secluded places can only be reached by boat.*

(16 km.) than either of the St. Georges, **Ágios Górdis,** an extensive west coast beach of ripples and sand bars, isn't nowadays so remote. The scenery rising up slopes behind Górdis is, however, still an enchanting blend of orchards, olive groves and vegetable farms.

A formidable construction in the shape of a big hotel has changed the isolated feel somewhat—but maps and roadsigns are as misleading as ever. The scene is dominated by a huge erect rock rising from the water at the south end of the beach.

Snorkelling and spear fishing are recommended off the rocks at the southern end of the long stretch of sand, and you should be able to engage a small boat.

The two alternative routes to Górdis go via SINARÁDES or KÁTO GAROÚNA, both unpretentious villages worth brief exploration. The two roads, winding through the verdant interior, are equally attractive. Public buses stop at the beach.

Named after a nearby hamlet, **Sidári** is a popular north coast beach and cove area featuring some fascinating sandstone and clay formations, curiously bevelled cliffs and the so-called CANAL D'AMOUR, a postcard favourite. The legend says that any young lady who swims or wades through this channel—actually a short sea passage worn through an outcropping—when the water is in shade will have her wish granted. Local girls seem blasé about it, but unmarried foreign hopefuls frequently venture through.

Sidári's best sand beach hasn't yet been over-developed. But you can eat, drink, dance and sleep close by in the village itself.

Getting to Sidári is half the fun: the drive features some of Corfu's best landscapes. Between the hamlets of MESARIÁ and ÁGIOS ATHANÁSIOS, the road coils through the most beautiful **olive groves** on the island. Thick ferns surround the contorted old trunks; here and there a cypress stands guard erectly over its neighbouring olives.

Time seems to stop in this incredibly tranquil part of the island, even in the simple villages along the way where photographers find it hard to resist quaintly colourful peasant houses. Less accessible behind high gates are some old Venetian manors.

Regular public bus services link Sidári with Corfu Town, 37 kilometres away.

From Sidári it's often possible to hire a caïque to take you to OTHONÍ, also called Fános, one of three small, dependant islands off the north-western coast of Corfu. Some think that Othoní may be Homer's Ogygia, the isle where Ulysses tarried for long years with that divinely seductive nymph Calypso (a bay here is named after her). Nowadays, only about 400 people live on the island, admired locally for its fishing grounds.

Signposts point the way to RÓDA beach, now easily accessible and with plenty of accommodation.

**St. Spirídon** (*Ágios Spirídon*), a semicircular strip located about as far north as you can go on Corfu, is so much smaller than the six other beaches described here that it only qualifies as half a beach. Walking the entire length takes no more than five minutes.

This is Corfu's "Greek beach"—but only on Sunday. Situated far off the normal tourist tracks, with a little chapel in honour of the island's patron saint and a small **39** restaurant, St. Spirídon is deluged by motorized Corfiotes on their day off. During the week, you'll find it deserted. Young children can frolic here in all security, the water stays shin-shallow over a ripply sand bottom for perhaps 200 yards.

Aside from this small sandy strip, the shore hereabouts is rocky. Spearfishermen often snare medium-sized octopus as well as the usual range of Corfiote inshore fish (see p. 93).

A salt-water channel at the end of the beach leads to the ANTINIÓTI lagoon, the favourite autumnal haunt of Corfu's duck hunters.

To reach St. Spirídon (43 km. north of Corfu Town) you take the attractive north-east coastal road 6 kilometres past Kassiópi just beyond the turn-off for Períthia. Look for a red dirt track off to the right, which may or may not be marked by a primitive sign for St. Spirídon. This winds through good olive groves for perhaps 3 kilometres on its way to the beach.

The nearest bus is 10 kilometres away in Kassiópi, but you can hire a boat to go to St. Spirídon and explore the rest of this quiet north coastal section.

# Corfu Town

Bustling, elegant, often charming, sometimes bewildering, this improbable port town is the island's proud capital and a welcome first experience for any visitor. It's called Kérkira in Greek, as is the island, but don't worry—everybody understands Corfu.

In the facial features of the 35,000 residents you'll detect traces of the Balkans, Italy, the Eastern Mediterranean: a reminder that Corfu has always been a maritime crossroads. Architecturally, Venetian, French and English styles blend bewitchingly with the Greek. The atmosphere is at once redolent of centuries past, yet familiarly modern.

## Around the Esplanade

Corfu lovers traditionally rave about the large green swath separating the Old Fort from the rest of town. You may wonder why when you see it, which you assuredly will because everyone seems to end up at its shaded café tables.

The Esplanade's greatest fame, of course, comes from its scrubby cricket field—still in use more than a century after British rule. On Wednes-

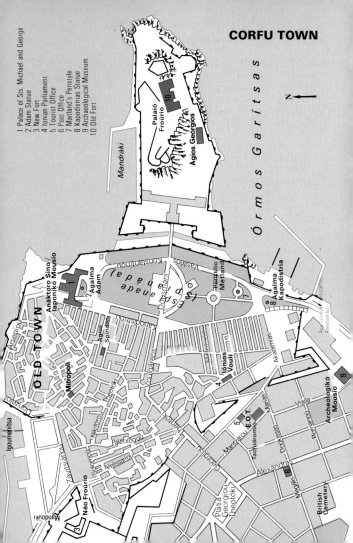

# CORFU TOWN

1 Palace of Sts. Michael and George
2 Adam Statue
3 New Fort
4 Ionian Parliament
5 Tourist Office
6 Post Office
7 Maitland's Peristyle
8 Kapodistrias Statue
9 Archaeological Museum
10 Old Fort

Palaió Froúrio

Ágios Geórgios

Mandráki

Órmos Garítsas

OLD TOWN

Anáktoro Síno/Iaponikó Mousío

Agalma Adam

(esplanáde) espianáde

Vasílios Konstantínou

Dousmáni

Kapodístriou

Teristilio Metland

Agalma Kapodístria

Ínpos Spirídon

Iríli Georgíou

Ións Liston

Mitrópoli

Theotóki

Iónios Vouli

Ghítelaz

Akademías

Arseníou

Kapodístriou

E.O.T.

Archeologikó Mousío

Nikifórou Theotóki

Mantzárou

Moustoxídi

Dórpfeld

Vrailá

Romanóu

Zavitsiánou

Paleológou

Melissárou

Guilfórd

Tachidromio

Igoumenítsa

Néo Froúrio

Plitá Georgíou Theotóki

Alexándras

Dossár

Mantzárou

Megális

British Cemetery

Mánduki

N

days and weekends during the season, you're likely to see visiting British teams at the wicket against local opponents, to the cheers and groans of hundreds of onlookers sipping cool drinks under the trees (see p. 96).

(see p. 96)

Nearby there are other mementos of Britain's Ionian sojourn: a yellowing and apparently infirm peristyle dedicated to the first high commissioner, Sir Thomas Maitland, and a primly old-fashioned green bandstand for Sunday concerts. Dominating the Esplanade is an impressive monument to Ionian-Greek union, surrounded by marble reliefs displaying the symbols of the seven islands. And there's a statue of Corfu's greatest son, Ioánnis Kapodístrias, who was free Greece's first president (1827–31). He also rates a major thoroughfare, which runs from his monument along the Esplanade.

All of Corfu Town's great occasions centre on the Esplanade. You'll doubtless hear it was established for strategic rather than aesthetic reasons: the Venetian garrison in the citadel insisted on razing the area to provide a clear field of fire against any enemy assault from inland. Nobody wants to

think how much blood was spilled here.

Many visitors like to linger along the **Listón** which fronts on the Esplanade. This graceful arcaded façade, patently inspired by the Rue de Rivoli in Paris, was the prime architectural contribution of the French during their brief occupation of Corfu. Today everybody meets everybody else at the Listón. But originally, it's said, only families on the élite "list" could walk under its arches.

Sprawled across the north side of the Esplanade is Corfu's colonnaded old **Palace of St. Michael and St. George,**

*Among Corfu's unlikelier aspects —an imitation French arcade and a museum devoted to oriental art.*

weatherbeaten yet imposing and unmistakably English. Sir George Whitmore was the architect responsible for this regency residence erected between 1819 and 1823. Originally it housed Britain's high commissioners, later the Ionian senate and members of the Order of St. Michael and St. George.

When the British departed, Greek royalty used the palace

as a residence. The staterooms are open to the public as well as the **museum** in an upstairs wing—one of the few *indoor* places well worth visiting on this *outdoor* island.

Though something of an oddity and about the last thing one would expect to find on a Greek island, the oriental collection of the Museum of Asian Art is quite remarkable. Rooms left of the grand staircase contain ancient Chinese funerary statuary and bowls, some almost 3,000 years old, as well as pottery and ceramics from half a dozen dynasties—Chou ritual bronzes, Ming buddhas and an entire cabinet full of tiny stoppered incense bottles. There's even some suggestively decorated T'sing dishware. The 8,000-piece collection was donated by Grigórios Mános, a former Greek diplomat.

Across the hall you'll find intricately designed oriental screens, Thai buddhas, two very ancient Khmer stone heads, bronzes of dragons and elephants, and hundreds of exotic statuettes in the collection of Hadjivassilíou. An assemblage of post-Byzantine Christian art (very inadequately labelled) includes many icons, some evocative frescoes and stone engravings.

For admission hours, see p. 118.

You won't find an identifying inscription on the bronze statue standing in a pool in front of the palace. But everybody in town knows that the figure, clad curiously in a toga now greening with age, is Sir Frederick Adam, Britain's second high commissioner and busy builder around the island. The pool and its little water spouts are there to remind people that Adam was the first to ensure Corfu Town an adequate water supply, with an aqueduct system still in use today a century and a half later.

## Old Town

By all means get lost in the Old Town—the fascinating maze of narrow streets, steep stairways and arched alleys pinched between the Old Fort and the Old Port.

As you wander along the flagstoned streets peeking into people's open houses and examining shop wares, you'll have the uncanny feeling

*Ageless and charming, Old Town conveys feeling of days gone by.*

you're in a mini-Venice. During their four centuries of rule, the Venetians were evidently homesick. This quarter—traffic-free, tall-walled, without pedestrian pavements—was as much like home as they could make it; they couldn't, alas, introduce canals and gondolas.

Nostalgia was only part of the story. In those days, the district between the old and new forts, comprising the entire town, was walled off for defensive reasons. Since Corfiotes weren't allowed to live outside the walls, the only direction they could expand their living quarters was up, hence the unusually high buildings.

Make sure you go beyond the few busy streets lined with shops that branch off from the Esplanade. Much of the Old Town's appeal is strictly residential, with laundry strung across alleyways, costumed old women on stools weaving

*Belfry of St. Spiridon, the island's highest, rises above Corfu Town.*

or watching babies, lean cats snoozing in tiny sun-splashed squares. You may come across an open musty cellar where men are tapping wine barrels; if you're offered a sip, it's polite to accept.

Photographers should be prepared at midday when blue-smocked school children swarm through the streets on their way home for lunch and siesta. And, almost any time of day, the view of the harbour from the marvellous little corniche road girdling the Old Town is worth a picture. The green island out in the water is Vídos, which has a large Serbian military cemetery*.

Meandering around the Old Town, you're likely to come across two churches much esteemed in Corfu. In a small chapel of solemn **St. Spirídon** lies the glistening silver coffin of the island's patron saint. The chapel is aglitter with hanging candelabra and full of the sweet smell of incense.

Except for special feast days and the four annual occasions when St. Spirídon's mummified body is paraded upright through town, the casket normally stays closed. Most of the faithful, who flock here in as-

tonishing numbers, are content to kiss the engraved silver lid. But for anyone requesting a special prayer direct to the saint, the lid will be opened.

Religious portraiture and some wooden panelling relieve the stark stone walls of this dimly lit church. In view of St. Spirídon's enormous popularity on the island, his church may seem rather small. But it does boast Corfu's tallest belfry, which probably seemed even higher 400 years ago when it was built. Like all Greek Orthodox churches, it's best at Easter, festooned with flowers and ablaze with lights.

Marvellously cool and a bit mysterious, **Mitrópoli** is the Orthodox cathedral of Corfu. It houses the headless remains of St. Theodóra, the island's second saint who was spirited out of Constantinople with Spirídon. She's greatly adored by the population even though she performs no miracles. Her silver reliquary, opened only once a year, stands to the right of the screen.

As the cathedral is just a few steps from the mainland ferries' pier, Greek voyagers often stop here to light a candle before or after a crossing.

There's a serene, Eastern beauty about this small church, amplified by the wel-

* The exiled Serbian army took refuge on Corfu during World War I.

47

ter of different-sized candle holders dangling from the ceiling.

If you notice a bearded man in black robes pottering about it's probably not the bishop but one of his assistants. All Orthodox bishops, priests and deacons have beards.

## Old Fort

Corfu has never been able to do without it, but you might feel you could. This storied Venetian citadel jutting bluntly out to sea on its promontory is something of an anti-climax when you visit it. Though students of military fortifications do seem to appreciate the citadel, parts of which may be 1,000 years old, only a lively imagination could evoke the heroics that took place in centuries past in this sturdy but now crumbling bastion of Corfiote defence.

It's undoubtedly best on summer evenings when they hold the sound-and-light performances. With appropriate fanfare, Corfu's history is traced—all the way back to Ulysses.

From the heights, there's a good panorama of Corfu Town and harbour.

The citadel's twin summits may have been responsible for the name Corfu: during the Byzantine era, it's said that the town was popularly called Stous Korphous (the two breasts) because of the promontory's peaks. The Greek *Kérkira,* however, derived from the much older Doric name *Corcyra.*

The starkly modern garrison chapel of St. George *(Ágios Geórgios)* has some unexceptional icons and recent religious paintings. Built by the British as an Anglican chapel, it became Orthodox when they left. Townspeople complain that the restoration done to repair World War II damage makes the church clash with the rest of the fortress.

## Archaeological Museum
*(Archeologikó Mousío)*

This pleasantly airy and modern museum has two of the finest works of antiquity ever dug out of the ground. You'll understand why archaeologists and amateurs flock to admire them.

The featured attraction, just over 2,500 years old, is the **Gorgon pediment** of a temple of Artemis. It's named after the ferocious, sculpted Medusa (one of the Gorgons) with wings at her back and shoes, serpents at her head and waist. She's flanked by Pegasus and Chrysaor, offspring born of her dying blood. Beside Medusa stand two alert lion-panthers ready for the command of this monster who turned all who gazed on her face to stone—or so the myth relates.

No other work of monumental Corinthian sculpture begins to match this. But the

*Local sights: pretty girls and carriages drawn by hatted horses.*

artist's identity is a mystery. The pediment, found in 1912 just south of Corfu Town, has undergone several expert restorations.

Not so colossal but every bit as fearsome is the **archaic lion** that lies menacingly atop a pedestal in the adjoining room. This remarkable sculp-

ture, also more than 2,500 years old, may have graced the tomb of a warrior back in the days when Corfu was struggling to win its independence from Corinth. Found on the edge of Corfu Town in 1843, the lion is considered to be one of the most beautiful ancient animal sculptures known.

The museum (Vraíla Street 5) is a few minutes' walk south of the Esplanade. For admission hours, see p. 118.

## On the Outskirts

The **Church of Saints Jason and Sosipatros** (*Ágii Iáson ke Sosipatros*) has an air of ancient Byzantium. This delightful limestone, brick and tile church fairly cries out to be photographed in its little flower-filled garden. It's slightly out of the way in the suburb of ANEMÓMILOS below Garítsa Bay.

It's the only surviving example on Corfu of the "inscribed cross" architectural style. As the friendly, white-bearded priest will try to make you understand, his church

*You still find ordinary, household items like tin pails made by hand.*

## Ulysses and the Maidens

Why argue? Local tradition insists that Ermónes Bay is the place where Ulysses dragged himself ashore after his shipwreck, fell asleep naked and salt-crusted, awakened to the chatter of maidens playing ball and met the fair Phaeacian princess Nausicaa. Homer's description of the site—the river cascading through pools to the sea —tallies with Ermónes, at least in the winter and spring. Besides, nobody has come up with archaeological evidence to the contrary.

Though often crowded nowadays, the beach has fine sand and some large shaved rocks for those who prefer spartan sunning. Food and simple facilities are close at hand.

The large rock resembling a human figure that dominates the bay is not Ulysses, but a pirate chief turned to stone for trying to steal a sacred icon from the local church. Or it could be a nun— depending on which of the local legends you prefer.

51

dates back to the 12th century, though earlier versions stood on the site during Corfu's Byzantine epoch (337–1204).

The whitewashed interior is immediately refreshing. The places of honour at the entrance go to two very beautiful 16th-century icons portraying Jason of Tarsus and Sosipatros of Ikonion, the militant saints credited with bringing Christianity to the island in the 2nd century.

A few minutes' walk from midtown Corfu, the serenely beautiful **British Cemetery** has special meaning for many British and Commonwealth visitors. Among the meticulously kept trees and bushes are graves with fascinating inscriptions dating back to the beginning of Britain's protectorate and those of British servicemen from both world wars.

# The North-East Coast

For many visitors, this part of Corfu bulging toward Albania holds special magic. Here are the limpid aquamarine coves and rugged, green mountain slopes that entranced English author Lawrence Durrell. His beloved "white house", now **52** partly converted into a *tavér-na,* still stands at the peaceful pebble-bottomed bay of KA-LÁMI. Civilization—a tarred road down to the water and some unsightly wire fences among the olives—has encroached only slightly on the marvellous landscape familiar to readers of *Prospero's Cell,* the Durrell work that has attracted so much attention to the island.

The dramatic beauty of north-eastern Corfu begins above the bay of ÍPSOS and ends near Kassiópi, a lovely drive over a winding but good road 20 kilometres long.

Dominating the entire region and providing the scenic high point is **Mount Pantokrátor**, Corfu's tallest peak. From just beyond PIRGÍ, a road of corkscrew curves and deteriorating quality goes up through SPARTÍLAS and STRI-NÍLAS all the way to the top, 2,974 feet above sea level.

Needless to say, the view is unbeatable. But even on a clear day, you won't "see forever", that is the more than 50 miles across the Adriatic to Italy.

*Priest stands proudly beside prized icon in Sts. Jason and Sosipatros.*

*Enigmatic Albania lies only a few miles away from this peaceful bay.*

What you will see is all of Corfu's sickle shape and, across that narrow channel, Albania with its mysterious Lake Butrinto. South, in the blue Ionian, lie Paxí and distant Cephalonia (Kefaloniá), two of Corfu's sister islands. (The antenna complex sharing the barren summit with you relays Athens television programmes around the island.)

Down at sea level, olive groves shelter a long pebbly and popular beach called BARBÁTI. Further north along the coast, pretty NISÁKI, where the water is a melodious medley of blues and greens, offers perhaps the best non-sand bathing on Corfu.

Little of this shoreline can be seen very well from the road winding high along on the slopes, but at various points you can go down for a swim. It's obviously best to explore by boat, something which can be arranged at most jetties.

After KALÁMI, where the Durrell house *is* visible from the road above, comes the twin bay of KOULOÚRA, barely large enough for a handful of fishing boats. Then the road knifes inland through less green hill and valley country, bypassing the north-eastern headlands, formerly a restricted military zone.

From this area, Albania is tantalizingly close—only 1½ miles away. But fishing boats, undersea explorers or innocent tourists who venture even a dozen yards into Albanian waters will unfailingly be challenged by armed patrol boats.

This watery boundary situation is particularly frustrating for archaeologists. Further south in the remarkably clear water of the Corfu-Albanian channel, a tempting collection of ancient amphoras has been spotted—the cargo of a long-sunken ship. Experts believe the amphoras date back about 2,400 years. The Albanians have made no effort to recover this treasure; nor will they permit anyone from the Greek side to do so.

The friendly seaside village of KASSIÓPI at the end of the north-east road is supposed to echo of past glories; in the summer it echoes with *bouzoúki* and modern electronic music. During an earlier heyday, Nero gave a fiddle concert here, or so they say, while other visiting celebrities included Cicero, Cato and Casanova (who apparently tried his amorous skills around the island with considerable success).

The only hint that Kassiópi was once an important port is a ruined medieval fortress. But tourists seem happy without the history. Swimming is off rocks or shingle, dining is open-air and simple, the atmosphere is completely casual. For an unspoilt, away-from-it-all village (population: 600), this is good value.

A number of public buses travel the 36 kilometres back and forth between Corfu Town and Kassiópi every day, stopping wherever passengers indicate. There are also guided excursions by boat.

For church buffs, the small, primitive hillside hamlet of ÁGIOS MÁRKOS (St. Mark), overlooking broad Ípsos Bay, is worth a brief visit. Near the village cistern stands a small yellow-grey church which, the caretaker asserts, is 500 years old. Inside, a lovely icon of Christ adorns a minute chapel to the right of the altar, probably painted about four centuries ago. Very appealing, too, is the icon of the Virgin Mary. The church is open mornings and evenings only. The view from the simple churchyard **55** would be the envy of most parishes anywhere. You reach Ágios Márkos by a sign-posted road winding up from the main Corfu-Kassiópi road right after Pirgí. If you're driving, watch out for the goats.

The stretch between Corfu Town and Pirgí supports an increasing number of hotels, seaside restaurants, grocers' and souvenir shops, especially at KONTOKÁLI, GOUVIÁ, KOM-MÉNO, DASIÁ and ÍPSOS.

## The Achíllion— Elisabeth's Folly?

If for no other reason, go for the view. This imperial-hide-away-turned-military-hospi-tal-turned-gambling-casino is the most controversial of all Corfu's sights. But almost every tourist visits it before leaving the island.

Whether or not you find the palace an architectural mon-strosity and the statuary a gro-tesque outrage, as others before you have done, you'll no doubt be impressed by the sweeping views from the Achíllion's carefully mani-cured hilltop gardens.

Back in the 1890s, the chronically morose Empress Elisabeth of Austria used to sit here in verdant solitude watching the sunrise. She had been captivated by the site and the island during a visit 30 years earlier, and as her mani-fold marital sadnesses multi-plied over the years in Vienna, her thoughts turned back to it. In 1890, she purchased the property and ordered a palace built that would be worthy of Achilles (hence the name). Neither the empress nor her several architects had a very clear idea of the harmonies of antiquity, and the result, in the so-called neo-classical style of the late 19th century, struck most observers as a most infe-licitous hodge-podge.

Poor Elisabeth only had a few years to enjoy the palace. She usually journeyed down in the spring and autumn, lead-ing an extremely secluded life. Then in 1898, a crazed anar-chist, Luigi Luccheni, assassi-nated Elisabeth in Geneva, Switzerland. She was 61. The Achíllion remains something

*Amazing array of statues peoples the grounds of Elisabeth's palace.*

56

of a monument to this unhappy monarch.

For a time, no acceptable buyer could be found. Then in 1905, Kaiser Wilhelm II of Germany visited Corfu and was taken by King George of Greece to see the Achíllion. The kaiser, happy to have a suitable base from which to pursue his archaeological hobby, acquired the palace in 1907.

Among all the statues scattered around the grounds only one is considered by experts to have possible artistic merit— the dramatic *Dying Achilles* by German sculptor Ernst Herter, acquired by Elisabeth

at an international art exhibition in Vienna in 1881.

The Achíllion's modest museum is composed of Elisabeth's chapel, a room filled with souvenirs of Elisabeth's years at Achíllion and the kaiser's room. Most attention here usually goes to an adjustable saddle on which Wilhelm, oddly enough, sat while writing at his desk.

Since December 1962, the Achíllion has functioned primarily as a casino, operated in large part by a West German concern.

During the day, visitors to the grounds and the downstairs museum pay a small

entrance fee. In the casino upstairs (see also p. 82), roulette, baccarat, chemin de fer and at times blackjack are the attractions.

While the Achíllion commands a fine view, you can look *down* on it and enjoy an even more spectacular panorama from Corfu's second tallest mountain, the 1,889-foot ÁGÏI DÉKA.

## South from Corfu Town

Nowhere else on Corfu can one see the impact of cement on natural beauty as graphically as at **Kanóni** (4 km. from the capital). Generations of earlier visitors knew the spot as a tranquil, green peninsula jutting south of the capital and featuring Corfu's most famous view, of two islets. It was a delightful walk or horse-carriage ride from town, popular with Corfiotes and camera-toting tourists.

No longer. New hotels and blocks of flats have brutally disfigured the landscape, although the builders' motives are hard to imagine—most Kanóni windows look out over the shallow, often murky Chalikiópoulos lagoon and the adjacent airport runway,

which supplies predictable sound effects.

The much-photographed islets, VLACHÉRNA and PONDI-KONÍSSI (Mouse Island), and the pleasant coastal scenery south beyond them remain intact. Presumably for that reason, tour operators still dispatch an endless stream of excursion buses to Kanóni. But the trip cannot be recommended.

Between the promontory and town lie the villa and ex-

*Perhaps Corfu's most photographed view: twin islets near Kanóni.*

tensive gardens of MON REPOS, closed to the public and mostly hidden from outsiders' view. Prince Philip, Duke of Edinburgh, was born here in 1921.

Built in 1831 as a summer residence by High Commissioner Adam, the villa later became the property of the Greek royal family. Corfiotes have been hoping, since the abolition of the monarchy, that Mon Repos will be opened to general viewing.

From nearby ANÁLIPSI (once the acropolis of the ancient town of Corcyra), you can see part of the Mon Repos grounds sloping down to the sea, as well as the still pleasantly verdant eastern side of the Kanóni peninsula. Archaeologists have established that the original 8th-century **59**

B.C. Corinthian city sprawled over much of this area.

Signs at Análipsi point the way down a rough track to the source of the locally famous Kardáki water. According to popular legend—and a sonnet by the poet Lorénzos Mavílis—any foreigner who drinks from this very old spring will forget his own country.

Probably the best example of what passes as "swinging" in the Corfu countryside is found at BENÍTSES, 12 kilometres south of the capital. This little seaside village thrives on the annual influx of foreigners who crowd the hotels, villas, cafés and restaurants and dance to the seemingly non-stop music. Amidst all the gaiety, the rather mournful little beach strip and second-class Corfu scenery seem to go unnoticed.

Continuing south the coastal road runs along the water until MESONGÍ. Here, near a stretch of narrow beach, are some of the island's proudest olive groves, with trees said to be well over 500 years old.

Below Mesongí, on Corfu's rather flat southland, the major attraction is Ágios Geórgios beach (see p. 36). Otherwise, this is olive, orchard and vegetable country. The main road passes through a few dusty, sleepy villages brightened by masses of flowers and an occasional, enthusiastic paint job. You may come across gypsies in caravans, a dog inevitably tied to each wagon. Down here in this part of the island, Corfu somehow seems hotter, drier and poorer. When you reach KÁVOS at the end of the road, it's hard to believe you've only travelled 47 kilometres from the capital.

Kávos offers delightful views of the mainland, across the Gulf of Kérkira, but the beach —like most on Corfu's east coast—is unexciting. Several outdoor seaside restaurants are located in and around the village, as well as dozens of holiday villas.

You should be able to negotiate a caïque trip from Kávos to the beautiful small island of Paxí (see p. 63), but don't expect to come back the same day.

There is a public bus service between Corfu Town and Kávos, and travel agencies conduct group excursions which include a stop for a swim and lunch here.

*Life proceeds at a gentle pace in the seaside village of Benítses.*

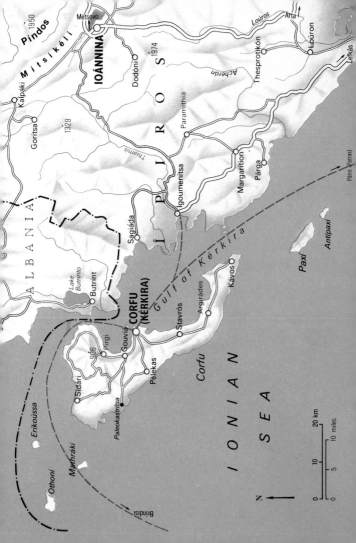

# Excursions

## Paxí (Paxos)

One of the most delightful island experiences in all of the Mediterranean awaits you just 10 nautical miles south of Corfu. Paxí (Paxos in English), the smallest of the seven principal Ionian islands, starts to seduce the visitor even before the boat docks: the sea here is astonishingly clear, its greens greener, its blues bluer than almost anywhere else in Greece.

This tiny, verdant island (approximately 5½ by 2 miles) has 300,000 olive trees and just over 2,000 inhabitants. Circe, the enchantress who detained Odysseus on her island and turned his men into swine, came from here (or so legend would have it).

It's perfectly ordinary behaviour to go barefoot on the whitewashed paving stones of the tiny villages. The gentle friendliness of the islanders seems almost otherworldly.

Paxí is proof that you can get away from it all without sacrificing all comfort. Though hotel accommodation is minimal, there are several hundred beds available for visitors in neat, clean, decently appointed houses. That's important, because with the somewhat erratic boat service—not to mention the charms of the island—many tourists will want to spend at least two nights.

Even on the briefest visit, don't miss the truly spectacular **sea caves** in the towering cliffs along the west coast. From your small boat, you may not see the seals which have long inhabited these cavernous depths, but you will see blue water that is totally dazzling in intensity.

Snorkelling or scuba-diving here is something you won't forget: the sea depth off these sheer rocks plunges from 30 to 100 yards, with fish of different sizes gliding in schools at different levels. You seem to be peering down into a breathtaking, blue eternity, and you can't help wondering what might suddenly emerge from the lowest fathoms.

Soaring out of the sea at one point along this mighty coast is a huge rock called **Orthólithos,** an appealing photograph. In the best Homeric tradition, a favourite modern Paxí tale relates that a Greek submarine hid in the largest of these caves, Ipapandí, during World War II, venturing out to conduct valiant operations. It's only wishful thinking. A submarine did call once at **63**

Paxí for repairs, though, and from such humble roots spring Ionian legends!

A boat trip around the island, immensely worthwhile, can be arranged easily from GÁIOS, the little quayside capital in the south, or LÁKKA, the picturesque mini-port in the north. The price will pro-bably have to be negotiated. During the season, more for-mal, large boat cruises may leave from Gáios.

As you'll see from the number of yachts docking here, Paxí can hardly be called "un-discovered", at least by the marine jet set. In recent years some well-known Britons have

## BERLITZ® GOES VIDEO – *FOR LANGUAGES*

Here's a brand new 90-minute video from Berlitz for learning key words and phrases for your trip. It's easy and fun. Berlitz language video combines computer graphics with live action and freeze frames. You see on your own TV screen the type of dialogue you will encounter abroad. You practice conversation by responding to questions put to you in the privacy of your own living room.

Shot on location for accuracy and realism, Berlitz gently leads you through travel situations towards language proficiency. Available from video stores and selected bookstores and Berlitz Language Centers everywhere. Only $59.95 plus $3.00 for shipping and handling.

To order by credit card, call 1-800-228-2028 Ext. 35.
Coming soon to the U.K.

# BERLITZ® GOES VIDEO – *FOR TRAVEL*

Travel Tips from Berlitz – now an invaluable part of the informative and colourful videocassette series of more than 50 popular destinations produced by Travelview International. Ideal for planning a trip or as a souvenir of your visit, Travelview videos provide 40 to 60 minutes of valuable information including a destination briefing, a Reference Guide to local hotels and tourist attractions plus practical Travel Tips from Berlitz.

Available from leading travel agencies and video stores everywhere in the U.S.A. and Canada or call 1-800-325-3108 (Texas, call (713) 975-7077; 1-800 661 9269 in Canada). Coming soon to the U.K.

*Travelview*
INTERNATIONAL
5630 Beverly Hill
Houston, Texas 77057

bought or taken villas for the season, but year-round foreign residents number a bare handful.

While it's easy enough to cover the entire island on foot, scooters can be hired, or for several persons a taxi is a reasonable proposition—with a built-in guide. As you're touring, you'll notice eight widely scattered stone structures resembling wartime pillboxes; in fact they're former windmills minus sails, oddities in a lovely landscape.

Between the hamlets of MAGAZIÁ and FOUNTANÁ is the island's largest olive tree—it takes five men with outstretched arms to embrace the huge twisted trunk. This giant stands in an incredible grove of 500-year-old trees, all still producing excellent olives faithfully every two years.

From the tidy hilltop cemetery at the Ágii Apóstoli (Holy Apostles') Church, the striking **view** of the chalk-coloured Erimítis cliffs is worth all the postcard photographs ever taken of them.

Although Paxí has nearly 80 churches, only about 50 are ever used these days—and then rarely—for lack of priests. The island's patron saint, Charálabos, seems to play second fiddle to Corfu's miraculous St. Spirídon. The most popular name for Paxiot boys is Spíros.

At LOGGÓS (often called LONGÓS), a minuscule port on the east coast, fishermen keep lively lobster and crayfish in sea pens awaiting almost daily shipment to Corfu where the fishing profession is declining as tourism increases. You should find a lobster meal on Paxí slightly less expensive than on Corfu, but it still won't be cheap.

Across the narrow sea channel opposite Gáios is the islet of PANAGÍA. Each Assumption Day, August 15, practically the entire population of Paxí goes over in a procession of small boats for a service at the chapel and a traditional serving of beef broth. For the rest of that day, the main square of Gáios is the scene of folk dancing and drinking, easily the greatest excitement of the year at this the social centre of the island.

Rare is the swimmer who can resist the limpid waters of Paxí. The island has no sandy beaches, though off the shingle strip at Lákka the bottom is

*The mighty rock of Orthólithos seen from the sea caves of Paxí.*

65

pure sand. But you'll find excellent swimming from flat rocks as well as a number of pebbly coves around the shoreline.

Even better is **Antípaxi** (Antipaxos), a totally unspoiled and wildly beautiful island 3 nautical miles south of Paxí. This vineyard-cloaked island has 55 houses (without electricity) but fewer than 20 permanent residents. A caïque trip there from Gáïos takes perhaps 40 minutes. Here, too,

the transparency of the water is incredible.

The only proper sand beach on Antípaxi is called VRÍKA, a small arc in a little cove. The fine sandy sea bottom here extends 8 yards out and then smooth white pebbles take over. The nearby bay of VOUTOÚMI has a similarly sandy bottom but only white stones along its coastal strip. Swimming at both is superb.

There's not a trace of civilization at either Vríka or Voutoúmi—meaning no food. But during the season a boat leaving Gáïos every morning for Voutoúmi returns in time for a late lunch. Otherwise, those hiring caïques take picnics.

Paxí, like Corfu, owes most of its olive trees to the Venetian rulers who paid bonuses to anyone planting them. Also like Corfu, it owes its glorious greenness to an abundant rainfall. As you stroll around, you'll see lovingly tended grape arbours and bougainvillaea in monumental profusion, not to mention cactus.

Though helicopters can land for emergency medical problems, you must get to Paxí by boat. From Corfu Town, there should be at least one public transport boat a day during the tourist season, perhaps a car ferry, perhaps a smaller passenger/freight ship. The trip can take anywhere from 2½ to 5 hours.

There may also be a more expensive one-day excursion from Corfu Town to Paxí and Antípaxi (perhaps to Párga on the mainland as well), returning in the evening. Finally, between Gáïos and Párga about 90 minutes away, there's a daily caïque service.

To really enjoy Paxí, a tourist from Corfu should plan to spend two nights—enough time to see island highlights and swim at Antípaxi. But beware: there's a compelling charm about the place, something in the relaxed atmosphere which has caused countless visitors to linger far longer than they intended.

## The Nearby Mainland

While you're hardly likely to develop "island fever" on Corfu, the mainland lies just 90 minutes away by ferry—and it's unquestionably worth a visit. Boats leave the Old Port in Corfu Town

*Black-robed, white-bearded priests are a common sight on the islands; the sunsets here can be stunning.*

about a dozen times a day in the summer. If you're lucky, dolphins will show off alongside during your passage.

You land at IGOUMENÍTSA, drowsy little gateway to Epirus *(Ípiros)* in north-western Greece. Right away you're face to face with some of Europe's most ruggedly magnificent scenery.

Driving inland through rarely explored mountain valleys, you'll most likely be obliged to slow down or stop frequently: large flocks of sheep and goats wander seemingly at will. For mile after mile, the only signs of civilization are the paved road itself and the odd shepherd's cottage off on a distant hillside.

The district capital, IOÁNNINA, is a lakeside mixture of old Turkish and modern Greek surrounded by high mountains. Here the fearsome Albanian despot Ali Pasha reigned supreme until he was beheaded, in 1822, on the monastery island sitting out in the lake.

A delicate minaret and a musty bazaar-like quarter of the city recall the long centuries of Ottoman occupation, which didn't end until 1913. A persevering shopper might find a worthwhile buy among **68** the thousands of silver and brass items displayed here. Smoked-cheese lovers should sample Metsovone or the other similarly named varieties brought in from the charming mountain village of Métsovo to the east.

Just five minutes beyond Ioánnina at the hillside hamlet of **Pérama,** you come to a superb speleological spectacle.

An eerie underground wonderland, almost a mile in length, awaits you. Many of the stalactites and stalagmites have names. And these incredible creations of nature often bear a striking resemblance to familiar things.

There are 19 types of mineral formation here. To add just one-half inch takes 60 years of the slow dripping process; thus it's no surprise to hear that the grotto is some 1.5 million years old. Among the cave's discoveries were the teeth and bones of a family of bears living here some 600,000 years ago.

It's standard practice to tip your guide, although his narrative and flashlight services are part of your entrance fee.

*Graceful minaret points skywards at Ioánnina; nearby, below ground, the spectacular caves of Pérama.*

theatre, lie in a beautiful valley south-west of Ioánnina.

The first Greeks-to-be came to Dodóni about 4,000 years ago. By the 14th century B.C., the dominant branch of this Indo-European people was the Selloi-Helloi, from which the name Hellas (Greece) derives. According to mythology, the word of Zeus was interpreted by priests at this hallowed place through the rustling of leaves on a sacred oak tree and various other means.

Temples were built, destroyed by invaders and rebuilt at the flourishing oracle until A.D. 390, when, it's said, barbarian Illyrians cut down the giant oak which had stood for more than 2,000 years. Rampaging Christians then levelled most of the "pagan" buildings, Goths and others drove residents away, and from 700 until 1875, Dodóni lay buried and all but forgotten.

Inspired by abundant tales of the oracle in ancient texts, Lord Byron toured the area early last century, but found nothing. Since the start of excavations, though, foundations of half a dozen temples and other sacred sites connected with the oracle have been uncovered. Coins, statuettes, pots, engraved stone frag-

### Dodóni

The region of Epirus loftily calls itself the "mother of Greece" because the ancient oracle of Dodóni pre-dates all the other oracles in the country, including that of Delphi. Remains of this sanctuary, most notably a large restored

ments and other Dodóni items are on display at the Ioánnina Archaeological Museum.

Every August a festival of ancient Greek drama is held at the Dodóni theatre, which can seat some 18,000 spectators. If you want to test the acoustics, stand in the centre of the 2,300-year-old theatre and speak very softly: anyone far up at the top benches will be able to understand you, and you'll hear the resonant echo of your own voice.

Dodóni's old oak trees whistle evocatively in the wind, while the surrounding violet and green mountains bespeak utter harmony and timelessness. If you feel uplifted or otherwise inspired in this tranquil cradle of Hellenic civilization, you won't be the first.

Dodóni, open daily from 9 a.m. until sunset, is free on Sundays; on the other days of the week there's a nominal entry fee.

*Magnificent setting for Dodóni, one of the oldest theatres in the world; below: the place to socialize, anywhere in Greece, is at an outdoor café.*

## ♟ Párga

Although this is the prettiest village on Greece's north-western coastline, it remains essentially unspoiled. As a stop-over on a mainland tour or for a longer stay, Párga is a sheer delight. The atmosphere here, the hospitable people, the whitewashed houses and paving stones, the casual *tavérnes* are totally Greek, conveying not a better but a different sort of charm from Corfu.

Párga offers splendid swimming, particularly at two long sandy beaches north and south of town, Líchnos and Váltos. Spear fishermen and snorkellers have all kinds of rocky depths to plumb nearby, while tourists can easily find fishermen to take them out in small boats for good catches.

Only in July and August is Párga very crowded with tourists, but even then it should be possible to find a room—if not at one of the many small

hotels, then in a private home. Among the groves of olive, orange and lemon trees, there's excellent camping as well.

With its little offshore islands in semicircular blue-green bays, a Venetian castle perched on a dominant promontory, and the comings and goings of brightly painted boats, Párga appeals to painters and photographers alike.

The village is an easy 48-kilometre ride south along the coast from Igoumenítsa. Good connections can be made between the Corfu ferries and public buses.

During the season there's a daily caïque service between Párga and the island of Paxí.

There's no regular organized tour that includes Ioánnina, Pérama, Dodóni and Párga. By car and with a very early start, it might be possible to see all these places in one hurried day, catching the last ferry back to Corfu from Igoumenítsa; but it would be far preferable to stay overnight at Párga.

A note of caution for drivers: some maps indicate a "direct" road from Dodóni to Paramithiá, which would seem to be the fastest way to reach Párga on the coast. It is not! This rutted, rock-strewn, gravel-sand-mud track twisting over 41 kilometres of wild mountain terrain must be one of Greece's slowest roads. The landscape is exceptionally beautiful, but the risk of damage to any but heavy-duty vehicles is great.

*The turquoise waters of Párga bay are dotted with picturesque islands.* **73**

# What to Do

## Shopping

Since Corfu is basically a one-town island, any major shopping you do will probably be in the capital. Small food shops called "super markets", newspaper kiosks and souvenir shops with various minor useful articles for sale cluster around hotels along the coast. Except for a brief siesta, such places usually remain open all the time, even on Sunday. They may not speak your language, but they'll no doubt try.

In Corfu Town, English is spoken in many shops. They're generally open from 8 a.m. to 1.30 p.m. and 5 to 8 p.m. (or 8.30 in summer), Tuesday, Thursday and Friday; 8 a.m. to 2.30 or 3 p.m. on Monday, Wednesday and Saturday. Practically everything in Corfu Town (except the odd pharmacy, restaurants, cafés and

discotheques) closes all day on Sunday.

Visitors should not expect to find too much in the way of bargains or treasures on Corfu: it is not a duty-free island and the range of locally made quality items is rather restricted. But you can buy some nice souvenirs to take home.

The Corfiotes claim with pride that their island is the "most European" part of Greece, and the age-old Mediterranean practice of bargaining is on the way out. Certainly, shops which sell food, wine, cigarettes and electrical appliances maintain fixed prices, and you should not expect to haggle.

In souvenir and gift shops, you'll find many of the owners or managers are multi-lingual, so you'll have no difficulty communicating. Here you'll find a bit of good-natured bargaining is tolerated. In any case, Greek shopowners are usually as hospitable as they are courteous, and prone to add a little gift to a purchase as a friendly gesture, and part of any deal.

If you do try your hand at bargaining, bear in mind that local profit margins have to cover the off-season, when the shop is closed, as well as the tourist months, so the room for negotiation is limited. Your chances of getting a discount should improve when you buy several items at the same time, however.

**Best Buys**
Corfu's most plentiful commodity—its olive trees—pro-

vides some of the best souvenirs. Local artisans carve a variety of attractive bowls, trays and oddments from olivewood which make fine gifts or additions to your own home. But of course there's more than wood to the venerable trees. Corfu's olive oil, of a quality and at a price you'll

*Corfu Town has all you need for a good picnic—including the basket.*

never match at home, comes in tins or plastic containers.

Reflecting a long and proud tradition of Corfu craftsmanship, handmade items of silver are enticing for the shopper. Look particularly for silver cake plates and hand-hammered containers for sweets, vaguely Venetian in design.

Along a few Corfu streets, you'll see an overwhelming array of handwoven and embroidered items. A typical and useful choice would be a *tagári*, a colourful woollen over-the-shoulder bag much in vogue on university campuses. Handwoven floor mats of wool and small carpets (the best from Epirus), tablecloths, napkins, aprons, skirts and blouses of lace and cotton (especially those woven in Corfiote villages) are always popular.

There's no better buy in this category than cotton needlework shawls and bedspreads; these generally must be ordered and will unfailingly be mailed to your home. Finally, you'll find those now familiar, heavy white stitched sweaters, made on Aegean islands, for sale here at interesting prices.

## Also Worth Considering

Other typically Greek souvenirs that are readily available include a strand of worry beads *(kombolóïa)*, records of those Greek songs you've heard so endlessly here, skewers for *souvlákia*—some very elaborate—and *bríkia*, the long-stemmed Turkish coffee pots.

Straw baskets similar to those sold elsewhere around the Mediterranean are prominently displayed in town. For children, there are dolls in Greek costumes and all sorts of toy figures.

In stationery shops you'll notice a curious legacy of bygone days: writing pads, account books, ledgers and so on are weighed on an old-fashioned scale and priced by the kilo!

Food to take home? That marvellous Corfu honey comes in sealed containers of various sizes convenient for carrying. Crystallized fruits, notably *koum kouat,* make a sweet gift. Another bestseller is nougat of almonds and other nuts. And don't forget about reasonably priced Greek liquors.

If you've fallen in love with *dzadzíki* or *taramosaláta,* you can pick up containers of processed, limited-duration versions even at the Corfu airport. The expiry date should be indicated. Though it's not quite the same as that served on the island, you can improve it at home with fresh ingredients.

*Shopping for souvenirs and gifts is more pleasant after sundown.*

# Principal Festivals and Holy Days

### January 1
On New Year's or St. Basil's Day *(Protochroniá)*, Corfiote motorists drop off presents at intersections around policemen directing traffic—from friendship, not as bribes!—and children receive just as many presents as at Christmas. Card games start the night before and continue until some time on New Year's Day; win or lose, the players then have good luck for the year ahead. A sprig of basil, named for the saint, may be offered a stranger as a gesture of hospitality.

### January 6
Epiphany Day *(ton Theofaniōn)*, when the waters are blessed throughout Greece. Small boys dive into the cold depths of Corfu harbour seeking to retrieve the cross blessed by the bishop. The one who emerges with it gets a prize, often a crucifix.

### Clean Monday
*Katharí Deftéra,* first day of Orthodox Lent. In good weather, everyone picnics. Only seafood, green pepper salad, beans, olives, *chalvá* (honeyed sweet) and special flat bread are eaten.

### Good Friday, Easter
*Megáli Paraskeví, Páscha.* No more colourful or unusual Easter celebration occurs anywhere in Greece. Huge throngs of Athenians, including high officials, and other mainlanders, invariably come to Corfu. Every church has its Good Friday procession. The most splendid starts after nightfall from the cathedral with the bishop, dignitaries and one of Corfu's famous bands.

On Holy Saturday morning, the patron saint, Spirídon, is paraded at length around town with spectacular pomp in honour of his miraculous intervention 400 years ago saving Corfu from famine. Then, at 11 a.m., police clear the main streets and suddenly from the upper storeys of houses are hurled pottery, old plates, vases, anything to shatter in pieces. The old Corfu custom (similar to Rome's New Year's Eve) is supposed to demonstrate anger at Judas's betrayal of Christ. This hour, known as the First Resurrection, is also the time for slaughtering the Easter lambs.

At midnight, when the bishop intones *Christós Anésti* (Christ is Risen), every electric light goes on, fireworks soar overhead, church bells ring and, most memorably, everyone lights a candle. Easter has arrived, and at least some of the pandemonium celebrates the end of Lent and particularly the severe fasting of Holy Week. On Easter Sunday all are invited to the military fortresses and police headquarters;

wine flows ceaselessly and men do the traditional Greek and Corfiote dances.

## May 21

Ionian Union Day *(Énosis ton Eptanison)*, marking the anniversary of the seven islands' joining Greece in 1864, occasions a magnificent spectacle in Corfu Town. A national leader lays a wreath at the Union monument on the Esplanade, cannons boom and jets fly past, as children, policemen, firemen, scouts, armed forces and many bands parade exuberantly for hours.

## December 12

St. Spirídon Day *(Agíou Spirídonos)*. All of Corfu's Spíros, which means well over half the male population, receive gifts and visitors on this, their name day. The body of the island's patron saint is stood upright at his church for three days so that everyone can kiss his velvet slipper.

# Nightlife

## Music and Dance

When the sun goes down, music comes into its own on this island which has always loved nothing better than a song and a dance. Almost every outdoor restaurant on Corfu has some sort of music

*Music reigns on Corfu, where you can clap, dance or dine out to it.*

to dine by or shout over. Often it's traditional Greek tunes, just as often the anything-but-traditional sounds of today's juke-box generation*.

Many tourists make a night of their evening meal, lingering on to watch or join the inevitable *sirtáki*, Greece's best-known group dance which can easily sweep up everybody in the *tavérna*. Familiar to those who saw *Zorba the Greek* and *Never on Sunday*, the *sirtáki* is great fun but not considered a totally serious dance by Corfiotes: you can still do it after drinking too much!

Other steps are much more challenging. You'll see the island's own two marvellously intricate dances, the *gastouriótikos* and the *agiriótikos*. In both, 15 or 20 women join hands forming a circle, enclosing two or three men who twirl and leap agilely about to the music of an accordion, a guitar and a fiddle. That trio of instruments produces the typically Corfiote music.

These and such national Greek dances as the circular *kalamatianós* and *tsakónikos* are taught to Corfu children at an early age—easy to believe when you watch their effortlessly precise and fluid movements.

The *zeibékikos,* always a crowd pleaser, is performed by a man or pairs of men. This is the one in which a dancer bends back and seems to pick up a table with his teeth as everyone claps to the music (actually, if you watch closely, he's taking the weight of the table on his chest and stomach).

Women or young girls alone do the lively, whirling Ágios Geórgios dance, particularly on Corfu village feast days.

You're also likely to see the traditional Greek butchers' *chasápikos,* which is similar to the *sirtáki,* and the sometimes wildly energetic sailors' dance, the *naftikós.*

The *sirtáki, zeibékikos, chasápikos* and *naftikós* are accompanied by that famous eight-stringed mandolin the *bouzoúki,* which for many foreigners has become—inaccurately—synonymous with all Greek music. Perhaps of Turkish or even more remote eastern origin, the *bouzoúki* is a comparatively recent import to Corfu. But, like much of the western world, the island has succumbed to the hauntingly beautiful melodies of Mànos Hadjidákis and Míkis Theodorákis. If your *tavérna*

---

* Note that both nightclubs and discos must close by 2 a.m.

doesn't employ a *bouzoúki* player, it will have a juke box, record player or at worst a radio to ensure that visitors will never be left in silence.

Impromptu dancing can break out anywhere. In addition, there are costumed performances of folk songs and dances throughout the season—the best at village festivals. More commercially, certain *tavérnes* stage such entertainment for after-dark tours organized by agencies or hotels.

## Other Sounds

With a vengeance, Corfu has forged into the discotheque era. The décor ranges from south seas to chic Parisian at the gaggle of electronic dancing spots which have sprung up on the island. Illumination and noise levels are similar to discotheques elsewhere, so patrons should feel immediately at home.

## The Vólta

You couldn't ask for better free-of-charge entertainment than Corfu's version of the Mediterranean evening stroll. Best seen along and near the Esplanade in the capital, this ritual is not just for self-conscious young boys and girls pretending to ignore each other while knowing perfectly well they'll be getting married eventually.

Middle-aged couples are out strolling in force, double-skirted old women push their grandchildren in prams, off-duty policemen walk with their backgammon partners, in fact almost everybody turns out for an hour or more before nightfall.

## Casino

The Achíllion casino, a 15-minute ride south of Corfu Town, is open from 7 p.m. until 2 a.m., offering roulette, chemin-de-fer, baccarat and at times blackjack (21). There is a fee for a single entry or you can get a weekly ticket. Take your passport. Men must wear jackets and ties.

## Cinema and Spectacles

Corfu's outdoor and indoor cinemas, concentrated in the capital, show foreign films, rarely of very recent vintage, with the original soundtracks and Greek sub-titles. Most films are English, French or American. The flourishing Greek cinema industry produces some excellent films.

# Wining and Dining

*Some seek their thrills in Corfu's casino, open till the early hours.*

The outdoor cinemas don't start until dark. Prices vary according to location but are always very cheap by international standards.

The Old Fort has nightly sound-and-light performances in various languages on summer evenings (see p. 48). There's more sound but less light at the once- or twice-weekly concerts at the bandstand on the Esplanade.

Rarely sophisticated, cooking on Corfu is honest and based on the many fresh ingredients available. You'll find most of the well-known Greek dishes on local menus, plus a few specialities unique to the island*.

In most hotel restaurants, however, you'll have scant chance to be adventurous: catering to large, mixed groups they tend to cling to that bland standard known vaguely as "continental cuisine", mildly enlivened by a few popular Greek dishes.

Helpfully, even simple *tavérnes* have supplementary menus in English and usually French. Service, however, is often exasperatingly slow. But here, as elsewhere in Greece, you're welcome to browse for your meal in the restaurant's kitchen.

If they're busy, nobody will be offended if you lift pot lids to see what's simmering or open up the refrigerated fish and meat compartments to inspect before you choose. As you point, a waiter, the own-

---

* For more information on wining and dining in Greece, consult the BERLITZ EUROPEAN MENU READER.

er's wife or the chef himself will note your order.

Right there in the kitchen is where you may well want to check on the credentials of the most expensive meal you can order on Corfu—lobster. You'll often be shown some of these creatures moving their appendages to prove they're alive. Your choice is weighed, because you pay by the kilogram. Then, instead of retiring to your table you might follow the advice of veteran lobster-eaters in the Mediterranean

*Some rewarding restaurants are to be found hidden in back alleyways.*

and stay put until your dinner goes into the pot. Corfiotes assume that even on this honest island, once in a great while, it's just possible that after being shown a live lobster, you might end up with a frozen one.

Corfu lacks any great variety of eating places, and distinctions are blurred between snack bars, *tavérnes* and restaurants. You won't, for example, find many of the stand-up *souvlákia* places so common elsewhere in Greece and so handy for a quick, tasty snack. Instead, meat on a skewer is normally served in a more formal restaurant.

Meal prices vary enormously, but in general one eats less expensively on Corfu than in most of western Europe. Menus list two prices next to each item available that day: the base price in the left column and the price including tax on the right. Government price control is in effect for each category of restaurant except de luxe. The total on a bill includes all service and other charges.

Diners normally leave between 5 and 10 per cent more for the regular waiter on the plate with the bill, and some drachmas on the table for the *mikró,* the little boy who

brings silverware, napkins and cold water and cleans away the dishes.

By Mediterranean standards, dining is early on Corfu. After 2 p.m. for lunch, or 9.30 at night, you're likely to find many items scratched off the menu or gone from the pots in the kitchen. But you're always free to linger at table over wine, fruit or whatever—particularly at outdoor seaside restaurants.

**First Courses**

Greeks like to order heaping plates of mixed appetizers, put them in the middle of the table and have everyone dig in, Chinese style. It would be a shame to miss any of the following hors d'œuvres, great Corfu favourites:

*Dzadzíki:* a chilled dip of yoghurt, pulverized garlic, grated or thinly sliced cucumbers, salt and a bit of olive oil and vinegar. It's eaten with the invariably fresh, crusty Corfu white or brown bread or even by the spoonful. The yoghurt used must be *sakoúlas,* not ordinary *giaoúrti.* Beloved around the eastern Mediterranean, *dzadzíki* is neither Greek nor Turkish, despite insistent claims. It actually originated in the Lebanese mountains.

*Taramosaláta:* well-known abroad, this is a pinkish paste of the roe of grey mullet (cultivated in Corfu's Koríssíon lagoon), mashed potato, olive oil and perhaps moistened bread. A squeeze of lemon enhances the flavour. It's eaten in the same fashion as *dzadzíki.*

*Kalamarákia:* small squid, usually fried in batter, served with lemon.

*Maridákia:* whitebait, generally fried and flavoured with lemon.

*Dolmádes:* grape (or cabbage) leaves stuffed with minced meat or rice, sometimes served hot with the familiar *avgolémono* sauce (chicken stock, lemon and eggs).

*Saláta choriátiki:* eaten as a starter, separately or with main courses, this "village salad" is as inevitable in Corfiote restaurants as everywhere else in Greece. Sliced cucumber, tomatoes, onions and perhaps green peppers, heaped in a pile, are topped with white *féta* (sheep or goat cheese) and black olives. You may want to mix up your own olive oil and vinegar. Incidentally, Corfu's restaurants serve pure oil directly from those olive presses you may see around the island, with no further processing. It's

## The Claw's the Thing!

Although menus all over the island translate *astakós* as "lobster", or *homard,* and the prices charged are certainly lobster-like, *astakós* is *not* lobster. It is saltwater crayfish, meaning it's clawless. Otherwise, it looks very much like lobster.

Practically never will a menu list lobster. But you *will* see some of these beauties, flexing their distinctive claws, at Corfu restaurants—though far less frequently than the *astakós.* The simple truth is that real lobster is becoming ever scarcer, so *astakós,* perhaps billed as "Mediterranean lobster", is sold instead.

Confusing the crustacean scene further is *karavída,* a similar but bonier variety. Some people think it has more tender meat than the other two. You should, however, pay much less.

Corfiotes, appalled at the current situation, say: "At these prices you don't eat the lobster; he eats you."

considered to be among the finest in the Mediterranean.

*Pastítsio:* baked macaroni and minced meat pie with white sauce and cheese, eaten either as a first or main course, as is the popular Greek dish ...*moussakás:* baked aubergine (eggplant) and minced meat pie with white sauce and cheese. Usually better at lunchtime, when it's freshly made.

**Fish and Seafood**

Fresh fish abounds, but even so restaurant prices will shock many visitors. Corfu is very proud of its only genuine seafood speciality, the pleasantly piquant *bourdétto:* white fish —it should be either *skorpiós* or *skilópsaro*—stewed in hot red pepper and olive oil, nothing else.

*Barboúni:* red mullet, the all-Mediterranean favourite, is probably the most popular fish on Corfu.

*Chtapódi:* octopus.

*Fagrí:* sea bream.

*Garídes:* prawns, perhaps served "Greek style"—cut up and simmered in a spicy tomato sauce with olives.

*Gávros:* anchovies.

*Glóssa:* sole, probably from Sicilian waters.

*Sardéles:* sardines.

*Soupiés:* cuttlefish.

**87**

*Sinagrída:* red snapper.
*Tsipoúra:* dentex.
*Xifías:* swordfish.

## Meat Dishes

*Soffríto:* slices of beef or veal stewed in a sauce of garlic and wine vinegar with a touch of black pepper, a Corfiot speciality.

*Souvlákia:* skewered veal or lamb grilled over charcoal, found everywhere and usually reliable, may also be called *shish kebab,* variously spelled.

*Keftédes:* Greek version of hamburgers or meat balls—made of minced beef or lamb, flavoured with grated onion, spices and herbs according to the chef's inclinations and energy.

*Kokorétsi:* spicy sausages of innards and herbs.

*Arní frikassé:* lamb stewed with green vegetables.

*Kotópoulo:* chicken, most often served boiled or stewed with vegetables.

In addition, you'll usually find steaks and chops; some outdoor restaurants offer little besides grilled meat and salad.

## From Eggs to Ice-Cream

Anywhere on Corfu or in Greece for that matter, sneer not at the lowly omelette *(omeléta);* it's always an excellent choice—plain, with cheese, ham, onion or whatever.

Corfu's seasonal vegetables include *angináres* (artichokes) which are served *laderés* (in oil) or in stews, *fasólia* (butter beans), and *fasolákia* (string beans).

The magnificent wild strawberries *(fráoules)* appearing in

May and June may be the tastiest treat in the Ionian. Other choice fruits include good seedless oranges, figs, apples, apricots, cherries, peaches, grapes and melons. Corfiotes share the national passion for nuts: *foundoúkia* (hazelnuts) are outstanding.

The cheese scene is rather uninspiring, though you'll find a pleasant Swiss-type Gruyère *(graviéra)*, an interesting sheep's milk cheese *(kefalotíri)* and, of course, *féta*.

Sweets are just that—and usually sticky as well. *Mandoláto*, an almond and honey nougat, has a big following as does the internationally known *baklavás*, honey and nuts between thin pastry leaves.

There's a running dispute in Greece over which section or island has the best honey *(méli)*. Corfu's rates very high on the list. Enthusiastically consumed, it makes a wonderful breakfast snack, poured onto the island's superior yoghurt *(giaoúrti)*.

Though not in the class of the Italian product, ice-cream *(pagotó)* in a few ordinary flavours is always available.

## Picnics

Freshly baked bread, juicily giant tomatoes, flavourful salami, a garlicky *mortadélla* (bologna sausage), cucumbers, tangy spring onions, Italianate cheeses, fresh fruits—ingredients for a picnic are easily available. For hikers or cyclers, rowers or anglers, budget-watchers or anyone too lazy to get off the beach, this is the solution.

## Beverages

At cafés around the island, and probably in your hotel, you'll automatically be offered Turkish coffee if you don't specify instant coffee—the usual alternative—or the Italian variety (now sometimes available). Despite its geopolitically unlikely name, the local brew, served with a glass of water on the side, is as Greek an institution as exists. When ordering, you ask for sweet *(éna varí glikó)*, medium *(éna métrio)*, or without sugar *(éna skéto)*. Let the coffee settle in your tiny cup before sipping; the grounds are not filtered out after it's boiled. Iced coffee, rarely available outside the capital and often somewhat tasteless, goes by the name of *frappé*. Tea *(tsái)* is usually good, English requirements being well understood on this island.

Bottled soft drinks—nota- **89**

bly lemonade *(lemonáda)* and orangeade *(portokaláda)*— are excellent. If you buy some for a picnic, save the bottles: the deposit may be as much as the price of the liquid. Also popular are small cans of grapefruit, pineapple and other fruit juices.

And, of course, Corfu is the only place in Greece where you can get genuine, 19th-century-style ginger beer. Locally known as *tzinzerbíra* (which may be pronounced "tsitsibeera" or "tsintsibeera"), it's served well chilled and is extremely refreshing in hot weather.

Greek lager-type beers, very popular on Corfu, should not disappoint most tourists. You'll also find foreign brews bottled under licence in Greece.

*Oúzo,* the national aperitif now making converts around the western world, is quite often taken neat *(skéto)* on Corfu; when you add cold water it turns milky—and less potent. Distilled from crushed grape stems, *oúzo* has a notably aniseed flavour. Some sort of *mezédes* (appetizers)—olives, cheese, a bit of tomato, crisps or potato chips—will often be served with your drink without extra charge.

Foreign aperitifs and liquors are available at much higher prices than Greek drinks.

Corfu produces a small quantity of local wines. But at hotels and most restaurants you'll usually be offered well-known mainland brands. If you're fortunate, however, as you wander around the island you'll find some open cask wine from Corfiote vineyards, which can be excellent.

Among bottled local whites, dry *Paloúmbi,* from the west coast hill town of Sinarádes, is probably the best. *Cápo Biánco,* from vineyards in the far south, varies in quality but is usually acceptable and inexpensive. *Corifó* wines, white and red, are dependable if unexciting. Far better is the burlap-wrapped *Robóla* (Calliga), a very satisfying, dry white from the sister Ionian island of Cephalonia. And you'll find Greek standbys like *Deméstica* (red and white) and *Sánta Hélena.*

*Retsína,* an acquired taste, is less popular on Corfu than elsewhere in the country. But you'll have no trouble finding this inexpensive pine-resinated white wine. It recalls the days before air-tight bottles when the Greeks transported their vintages in casks sealed with resin (which seems also to have acted as a preservative). Greeks may tell you that *retsina* helps digestion and rarely causes hangovers.

Corfu's red wines vary each season but normally are undistinguished. Most diners will prefer mainland reds like *Himéttus* or *Bácchus,* both lighter than local counterparts. *Castél Daniélis,* a noted red from Patras, is often available.

*Theotóki,* once considered among the premier wines of Greece and a source of considerable pride to Corfiotes, has long since lost its reputation. You may still see it occasionally on the island, at remarkably inappropriate prices.

For middle-of-the-spectrum drinkers, there are such rosé wines as *Kokkinéli* and *Rodítis,* better when served simply chilled instead of taken from a freezing compartment.

Greek vermouths and brandies have improved in recent years, but don't expect French quality.

The Ionian islands are known for their liqueurs. Corfu's inescapable speciality is *koum kouat,* a syrupy confection produced from miniature oranges that grow here, far from their native Japan. *Soumáda,* a popular almond cordial, may be drunk like *oúzo,* by adding water.

As for mineral water, Europeans won't write home about the Corfu varieties, but they're acceptable (usually flat, not bubbly). On the other hand, perfectly good, cold tap water is automatically served everywhere.

*Built for olives, this machine has been pressed into service on grapes.*

# Sports

With Corfu's marvellous climate, it's certainly possible to stay outdoors ten or twelve hours every day of your holiday. But one immensely important warning: this sun can be treacherous—it bakes white skins crimson in an amazingly short time. And that's just as true under a light cloud cover or haze as under clear blue skies. Few "tanning" lotions give total protection, so be very careful for the first few days.

Aside from sun bathing, aquatic sports are overwhelmingly the most popular recreational activity on Corfu. Prices for sports equipment and activities can be found on page 101.

## Swimming

The island's sometimes rocky, sometimes sandy, now flat then hilly coastline offers every imaginable swimming possibility.

As a general rule, Corfu's western and northern shores tend to have more surf than the eastern coast which faces the mainland, and the best sandy beaches front on the open Ionian (see p. 32). Until mid-summer, the water at Paleokastrítsa and other west-ern swimming areas is cooler than the rest of the island.

Only at or around Corfu Town (notably Garítsa Bay and the port areas) should swimming be avoided—because of pollution—though you may see intrepid bathers even here.

The number of beach areas with organized facilities and lifeguards is small but growing. You'll be able to tell, or somebody will pass the word, if there's any reason for special care while swimming—currents or breezes acting up, or the extremely rare sight of a shark close enough inshore to matter.

*NB:* Sunbathing and swimming in the nude are considered punishable offences, but toplessness is the rule in tourist resorts.

## Snorkelling and Skin-Diving

Fish are abundant around Corfu. Among the island's countless rocky inlets snorkelling and skin diving are often excellent and gastronomically rewarding (see p. 93). You'll find some fascinating small sea grottoes along the west coast as well as offshore rocks worth investigating. Don't be put off by eel grass at certain east coast points: some of the most colourful fish lurk in these shallows.

A scuba-diving school operates at Paleokastrítsa during the season, offering a two-week course with Greek- and English-speaking instructors. There are extended boat trips for advanced divers. A health certificate (obtainable from a Corfu doctor) is required for students.

### Fishing

Day and night, you'll find fabulous fishing all round the island. You won't need a licence, and there's no problem about hiring equipment or a boat. Dentex, eels, ink-fish, octopus, many white fish, sea bass and even crustaceans can be caught here, if you're lucky, plus many species that don't seem to have English equivalents. Local boatmen will take you out at any hour.

So abundant and hungry are the fish in Corfu's waters that many a rank amateur soon feels like a professional angler.

### Boating

Undoubtedly the best way to enjoy the coastline is by boat. You'll find everything from a peddle-it-yourself boat to a yacht for hire on Corfu, by the hour, the day, the week.

All categories of motor boats from a small five-horse-power outboard to a ten-metre caique with inboard motor and two crew members can be rented at rates varying according to size, usually with the cost of petrol included.

*For this fast-moving sport you need balance, muscles and a breeze.*

As for sailing boats, both two-person sailing dinghies and a one-person model for the ever-more-popular windsurfing can be hired.

Full sailing boats are also available but a proficiency certificate is required. Some hotels give sailing lessons.

## Yachting

On Corfu, as all over Greece, yachting is booming. With more than 1,000 yachts now calling at the island each year, this sport has become a major preoccupation of tourist officials.

Corfu port is already a class "A" yachting station with reserved mooring for several dozen vessels, dockside supply facilities for water, fuel and provisions. A large new 300-berth marina is planned at Gouviá; Paleokastrítsa has less elaborate facilities.

Conveniently for skippers travelling from Yugoslavia or Italy, Corfu is one of the country's few designated "entry-exit" ports where the obligatory transit log for every yacht may be obtained. This permits free sailing throughout Greek waters.

## Windsurfing

Boards and sails are available for hire at nearly every beach on the island where the right conditions prevail.

## Water-Skiing

If you don't already know how, Corfu has eight schools where you can learn to water-ski: Ipsos bay, Mesongí, Nisáki, Pérama and Benítses, all on the eastern shoreline where the sea is less choppy. Many hotels and seaside restaurants also offer water-skiing to all comers. However, this is not a cheap sport.

## Golf

Here's where your golf really can be legendary! Where else could you tee off within sight of the place where Ulysses purportedly met Nausicaa? Just inland from Ermónes Bay, Corfu's 18-hole course draws golfers from hotels all over the island. With fairways kept lush by an automatic watering system and spongy greens that hold the ball, the course plays rather slowly. That pleases professionals and

amateurs alike. But there's no cheering about a devilishly meandering stream which comes into play on 16 holes!

Professional lessons are given by qualified pros; it's best to book ahead. The staff of the well-equipped pro shop speak English. If you've come without your clubs, all the necessary paraphernalia can be rented here. Anyone can play.

## Tennis

If your hotel doesn't have courts, the Corfu Tennis Club, oldest in Greece, welcomes all visitors, but only in the morning from 8 a.m. to noon; the evening is reserved for club members. Founded, in 1896, the club, at Romanoú 4 in Corfu Town, possesses four asphalt courts. They can be hired by the hour but, as a rule, you may not reserve them in advance. You may rent a racket or take a lesson here. Every August there's an international tournament.

## Hunting

The season runs from August 25 until March 10. Tourists wishing to shoot should first notify the Aliens Police in Corfu Town and then get their licence from the Forestry

Department at Diikitírion. A licence, good for two weeks, is valid all over Greece.

Snipe, woodcock, duck and hare are usual targets on Corfu; migrating turtle doves attract hunters for about two weeks each September. You'll get all kinds of advice about the best shooting locations, but there's no disputing the fact that ducks abound in the marshy flatland surrounding the Korissíon lagoon.

*The field is rough and the pitch is concrete but nobody seems to mind.*

## Hiking and Walking

If you've a mind to, you can climb Corfu's tallest peaks, Pantokrátor (2,972 feet) and Ágii Déka (1,889 feet), or any of the dozens of other less challenging hills around the island.

Wherever you climb, hike or stroll, you'll probably have company, as Corfu has always attracted bevies of hardy nature lovers. If you're hiking overland rather than on the road, boots are wise since Corfu does have a variety of snakes, most of them harmless.

## Cricket

As if it were the most ordinary thing in the world to do on a Greek island, cricketers calmly perform at frequent intervals on Corfu Town's Esplanade. They've been doing it, complete with curiously Corfiotized English cricket expressions, ever since the Union Jack was hauled down here in 1864. Throughout the season, there are matches, mostly involving visiting British sides and often attracting baffled spectators as well as the regular local fans. But tourists wishing to play (Saturday's the likeliest time), should have their hotel receptionist make arrangements.

# BLUEPRINT for a Perfect Trip

## How to Get There

The details given below were correct at the time of going to press but as travel conditions, reductions and special fares change constantly, a knowledgeable travel agent should be contacted for the latest information.

## BY AIR

### Scheduled Flights

Though some European airlines fly directly to Corfu, most regularly scheduled flights are routed via Athens. Olympic Airways operates daily between Athens and Corfu, a 35-minute trip.

### Charter Flights and Package Tours

**From the British Isles:** There is a wide selection of package tours to Corfu, both in summer and winter. Prices vary depending on whether the flight is on a scheduled or a charter airline and on the kind of accommodation. Most travel agents recommend cancellation insurance, a modestly priced safeguard—you lose no money if illness or accident forces you to cancel your holiday.

**From North America:** In addition to the economical charter flights arranged by clubs or associations for their members and immediate families, low-cost plane travel is now available to the public at large. The least expensive is the Advance Booking Charter (ABC), which must be reserved and paid for a number of weeks in advance. If no flight is available to the right destination at the right time, you might consider flying ABC to a European gateway city and continuing to Corfu on your own.

## BY SEA

In summer, there is daily car-ferry service from Brindisi, Italy, leaving at night and arriving in Corfu the following morning. The main ferry lines to the Greek mainland connect Corfu to Patras and Igoumenítsa (a two-hour trip).

## BY ROAD

The normal route is from Dover to either Ostend or Zeebrugge, continuing to mainland Greece on the major routes skirting Brussels, Munich, Belgrade and Niš. From eastern and northern Greece there's a good road through Métsovo to Ioánnina and then down to Igoumenítsa (local ferry on to Corfu), or you could travel through Italy, taking a car ferry directly to Corfu.

Europabus services offer excursions from London and continental Europe to Athens.

## BY RAIL

The most direct route passes through Paris and Bern to Italy (Brindisi or Ancona) where you get the ferry to Corfu. It's also possible to travel via Brussels, Munich, Belgrade and Athens—a three-day train ride from London to Corfu.

**Eurailpass:** Anyone except residents of European countries can travel on a flat-rate, unlimited-mileage ticket valid for first-class travel anywhere in continental western Europe. You must sign up before leaving home. The Eurail Youthpass, available only to those under 26, buys second-class travel at a cheaper rate.

Both **Inter-Rail** and **Rail Europ Senior** tickets are valid in Greece.

# When to Go

In July and August, Corfu has the most sunshine, the highest air temperature, the warmest sea, the least rain and—the most tourists. All things considered, it's probably best to go between mid-May and late June or from early September to mid-October.

December is Corfu's rainiest month, January its coldest, but even during these mid-winter doldrums, the climate is temperate by western European or North American standards. Except at the height of summer, rainwear is worth taking to Corfu.

|  |  | J | F | M | A | M | J | J | A | S | O | N | D |
|---|---|---|---|---|---|---|---|---|---|---|---|---|---|
| **Air** | °C | 10 | 10 | 12 | 15 | 19 | 24 | 27 | 26 | 23 | 19 | 15 | 12 |
| **temperature** | °F | 50 | 50 | 54 | 59 | 66 | 75 | 81 | 79 | 73 | 66 | 59 | 54 |
| **Sea** | °C | 15 | 15 | 15 | 16 | 18 | 21 | 24 | 25 | 24 | 21 | 19 | 18 |
| **temperature** | °F | 59 | 59 | 59 | 61 | 64 | 70 | 75 | 77 | 75 | 70 | 66 | 64 |
| **Daily hours of sunshine** |  |  | 5 | 6 | 7 | 7 | 9 | 10 | 11 | 12 | 9 | 6 | 4 | 3 |

Figures shown are approximate monthly averages.

# Facts and Figures

Although much of the information given below can be found in various sections of our guide, key facts are grouped here for a quick briefing.

**Geography:** Corfu *(Kérkira)* is the northernmost and second largest of the major Ionian Islands, with an area of about 640 square kilometres (250 square miles), and lies at the entrance to the Adriatic Sea. Together, the islands of Corfu, Paxí, Levkas, Cephalonia, Ithaca and Zakinthos form the westernmost boundary of Greece. It reaches a length of ca. 60 km. (40 miles) and a width of 30 km. (18 miles). The northern part of the island is only about 2 km. (1.5 miles) from the Albanian Coast, and the southern tip about 8 km. (5 miles) from the Greek mainland. The highest point is Mount Pantokrátor at 906 metres (2,974 feet) in the north-eastern part of the island.

**Population:** Ca. 115,000.

**Major town:** Corfu (*Kérkira,* 35,000).

**Government:** Greece is a presidential parliamentary republic. The country is divided into 10 regions, which are subdivided into more than 50 administrative districts or prefectures *(nómi),* of which Corfu comprises one. Each *nómos* is administered by a local governor or nomarch who is appointed by the central government in Athens, and each *nómos* is represented in Parliament by deputies, the number depending on the population of each individual district.

**Economy:** Corfu's main sources of income are tourism and agricultural products such as olives, wine, grapes, oranges and grain, in addition to fisheries and stock raising.

**Religion:** More than 95% of Greeks belong to the Orthodox Church, headed by the Patriarch of Constantinople and Archbishop of Athens.

# Planning Your Budget

To give you an idea of what to expect, here are some average prices in Greek drachmas (drs.). However, take into account that all prices must be regarded as *approximate,* because inflation is running high.

**Airport transfer.** Bus to Corfu Town 50 drs., taxi 250–300 drs.

**Baby-sitters.** 500–700 drs. per hour.

**Bicycle and motorscooter hire.** *Bicycles* 400 drs. per day, 2,000 per week. *Motorscooters* 1,000 drs. per day, 5,000 per week.

**Buses.** Corfu Town to Sidári 145 drs., to Paleokastrítsa 105 drs., to Ípsos 65 drs., to Kávos 185 drs.

**Camping** (per day). 240 drs. per person, 250 drs. for tent, 220 drs. for car, 360 drs. for caravan (trailer), 120 drs. for scooter.

**Car hire** (international company, high season). *Seat Fura* 1,970 drs. per day, 25 drs. per km., 34,650 drs. per week with unlimited mileage. *Nissan Sunny* 2,950 drs. per day, 31.20 drs. per km., 46,900 drs. per week with unlimited mileage. Add insurance and 20% tax.

**Cigarettes** (packet of 20). Greek brands 40–100 drs., imported 150–180 drs.

**Entertainment.** *Bouzoúki* music (including an *oúzo* and *merzédes*) 1,500 drs., discotheque from 500 drs., *casino* 150 drs. for single entry, *cinema* 150–200 drs.

**Guides.** 5,000 drs. per day (7 hours), 3,000 drs. per half-day.

**Hairdressers.** *Woman's* shampoo and set 1,200–1,400 drs., permanent wave 2,200–2,500 drs. *Man's* haircut 500–600 drs.

**Hotels** (double room with bath, high season). De luxe 10,000–17,000 drs., Class A 5,500–7,000 drs., Class B 4,500–5,500 drs., Class C 2,800–3,500 drs., Class D 1,700–2,500 drs.

**Meals and drinks.** Continental breakfast 150–300 drs., lunch/dinner in fairly good establishment 800–1,500 drs., coffee (instant) 100 drs., Greek brandy 100–200 drs., gin and tonic 350 drs., beer 100–150 drs., soft drink 50–80 drs.

**Sports.** *Dinghy* 2,500 drs. per day. *Yacht* from $90 per day. *Water-skiing* 1,000 drs. for 10 minutes. *Golf* green fees 2,200 drs. per day, 8,800 drs. per week, clubs 1,000 drs. per day, pull cart 300 drs. *Tennis* 400 drs. per person per hour.

**Taxis.** Corfu Town (with return) to Kávos 5,000 drs., to Dasiá 2,000 drs., to Sidári 5,000 drs.

# An A–Z Summary
# of Practical Information and Facts

> A star (*) following an entry indicates that relevant prices are to be found on page 101.
>
> Listed after most entries is the appropriate Greek expression, usually in the singular, plus a number of phrases that should help you when seeking assistance.

**A** **AIRPORT\*** (ΑΕΡΟΔΡΟΜΙΟ—*aerodrómio*). Barely a mile from the capital, Corfu's lagoon-side airport has a modern runway capable of handling all but the largest jets.

There should be a handful of porters around to carry bags the few steps to buses and taxis. There's no charge, but a small tip would be appropriate. Charter or package-tour luggage is usually put directly aboard coaches.

The terminal building features modern toilets and snack bars as well as a duty-free shop and souvenir, packaged food, wine and leather shops, car rental counters and a newspaper stand.

The currency-exchange office at the airport is open daily from 9 a.m. to 11 p.m.

Olympic Airways operates a regular bus service between the airport and the town centre. Major hotels have their buses meet flights carrying clients.

| | |
|---|---|
| Porter! | **Achtofóre** |
| Take these bags to the bus/taxi, please. | **Pigénete aftés tis aposkevés sto leoforío/taxi, parakaló.** |

**ALPHABET.** See also Language, and box on page 13. The exotic letters of the Greek alphabet needn't be a mystery to you. The table below lists the Greek letters in their capital and small forms, followed by the letters they correspond to in English.

| A | α | a | as in bar |
| B | β | v | |
| Γ | γ | g | as in go* |
| Δ | δ | d | like th in this |
| E | ε | e | as in get |
| Z | ζ | z | |
| H | η | i | like ee in meet |
| Θ | θ | th | as in thin |
| I | ι | i | like ee in meet |
| K | κ | k | |
| Λ | λ | l | |
| M | μ | m | |
| N | ν | n | |

| Ξ | ξ | x | like ks in thanks |
| O | o | o | as in bone |
| Π | π | p | |
| P | ρ | r | |
| Σ | σ, ς | s | as in kiss |
| T | τ | t | |
| Y | υ | i | like ee in meet |
| Φ | φ | f | |
| X | χ | ch | as in Scottish loch |
| Ψ | ψ | ps | as in tipsy |
| Ο/Ω | ω | o | as in bone |

| OY ου | | ou as in soup |

Stress, a very important feature of the Greek language, is indicated in our transcription by an accent mark (´) above the vowel of the syllable to be emphasized.

**ANTIQUITIES** *(archéa)*. Antiquities may be exported only with the approval of the Greek Archaeological Service and after paying a fee. Anyone caught smuggling out an artefact may receive a long prison sentence and a stiff fine, and the item will be confiscated. Travellers purchasing an antiquity should have the dealer obtain an export permit.

**BABY-SITTERS\*.** If you need a baby-sitter, inquire at the hotel reception desk and arrangements will be made, providing you give sufficient warning.

Actually, children are accepted almost everywhere at any time on Corfu. Most Corfiotes take them along whenever they go out, even to late-night restaurants.

| Can you get me/us a baby-sitter for tonight? | **Boríte na mou/mas vríte mía "baby-sitter" giapópse?** |

---

* except before **i-** and **e-**sounds, when it's pronounced like **y** in yes

**B**  **BICYCLE and MOTORSCOOTER HIRE*** *(enikiásis podilóton/moto-podilóton).* Practically everywhere tourists stay on the island there are rental agencies, with rates varying widely. Shopping around is wise. Bargaining may be possible off-season, and if you're hiring a number of machines or seeking one for a long period, you should definitely get a lower rate. Agents usually charge a non-negotiable insurance fee for all motorized two-wheelers.

| | |
|---|---|
| What's the rental charge for a full day? | **Póso kostízi giá mía iméra?** |

**BUSES*** *(leoforío).* The island's public bus service, centred on Corfu Town, is good and not expensive. Timetables are displayed at bus-stops (ΣΤΑΣΙΣ—*stásis*) in the capital and are also available from the National Tourist Organization (see TOURIST INFORMATION OFFICES). There are no all-night bus services.

Keep your ticket, as inspectors may come aboard along the route. In Corfu Town, buses for various points leave from the Cricket Ground, Platía Theotóki and the New Fort Square (see map on p. 41).

| | |
|---|---|
| When's the next bus to …? | **Póte févgi to epómeno leoforío giá …?** |
| single (one-way) | **apló** |
| return (round-trip) | **me epistrofí** |

**C**  **CAMPING*** (ΚΑΜΠΙΝΓΚ—*"camping"*). There are 13 official, organized campsites on the island. Camping is forbidden elsewhere. All sites have the usual facilities and are open at least from April to October. Some offer water-skiing and other extras.

For the list of sites and their facilities, contact the EOT office in Corfu or the National Tourist Organization of Greece in your country (see TOURIST INFORMATION OFFICES).

| | |
|---|---|
| Is there a campsite near by? | **Ipárchi éna méros giá "camping" edó kondá?** |

**CAR HIRE*** (ΕΝΟΙΚΙΑΣΕΙΣ ΑΥΤΟΚΙΝΗΤΩΝ—*enikiásis aftokiníton).*
**104** See also DRIVING IN GREECE. There are more than a dozen car hire

firms on Corfu. As everywhere in Greece, it's not cheap to hire a car, but it is sometimes possible to discuss special terms with local firms.

Deposits are often waived for credit card holders and members of large tour groups who may also obtain a small discount. Though the International Driving Permit is legally obligatory for foreign motorists *hiring* a car in Greece, firms in practice accept virtually any national licence, stipulating that it must have been held for at least one year. Depending on the hiring firm and the model, minimum age for renting a car varies from 21 to 25.

| | |
|---|---|
| I'd like to hire a car (tomorrow). | **Tha íthela na nikiáso éna aftokínito (ávrio).** |
| for one day/a week | **giá mía iméra/mía evdomáda** |
| Please include full insurance. | **Sas parakaló na simberilávete miktí asfália.** |

**CIGARETTES, CIGARS, TOBACCO\*** *(tsigára; poúra; kapnós).* The sign to look for is ΚΑΠΝΟΠΩΛΕΙΟ *(kapnopolío).* Greek cigarettes, manufactured of good quality tobacco and generally mild, are far cheaper than the few foreign brands (manufactured under licence in Greece) available around the island.

You can try the local variety of cigars without any qualms, or find your regular Dutch brand without any problems.

Pipe tobacco, both local and imported, is also easily obtainable, though the latter may cost three times as much.

| | |
|---|---|
| A packet of .../A box of matches, please. | **Éna pakéto .../Éna koutí spírta, parakaló.** |
| filter-tipped | **me filtro** |
| without filter | **chorís filtro** |

**CLOTHING** *(rouchismós).* Unless you want to gamble at the casino, you can leave ties and fancy dresses at home; clothing is almost always casual on Corfu. After dark, even in mid-summer, women may occasionally appreciate a wrap or shawl, men a jacket or sweater.

Since it does rain from time to time in Corfu (see WHEN TO GO, p. 100), some sort of protective coat or at least an umbrella is a very good idea. But, except for winter, make all your clothing lightweight. Cotton is preferable to synthetics in hot weather.

Sensible walking shoes are a must, especially heavy boots for cross-country hiking; plastic or rubber bathing slippers are useful for stony beaches. Rubber-thonged sandals are sold on the island.

| | |
|---|---|
| Will I need a jacket and tie? | **Tha chriastó sakáki ke graváta?** |
| Is it all right if I wear this? | **Tha íme endáxi an foréso aftó?** |

## COMMUNICATIONS

**Post offices** (ΤΑΧΥΔΡΟΜΕΙΟ—*tachidromío*) handle letters, stamp sales, parcels and money orders, but not telegrams and phone calls. They can be recognized by a yellow sign reading ΕΛ.ΤΑ.

**Hours** are usually from 7.30 a.m. to 8 p.m., Monday to Friday (till 2.30 p.m. for money orders and parcels).

In tourist hotels, the receptionist will usually take care of dispatching mail.

Registered letters and parcels going out of Greece are checked before being sent, so don't seal them until you have presented them at the post office desk.

Stamps may also be bought at most places which sell postcards. Note that Greek letter boxes are painted yellow.

**Poste restante (general delivery).** If you don't know ahead of time where you'll be staying, address your mail poste restante:

> Mr. John Smith
> Poste Restante
> Corfu
> Greece

In Corfu Town, you can pick it up from the main post office at the corner of Alexándras and Megális. Take your passport with you for identification.

**Telegrams** (*tilegráfima*) and **Telephone** (*tiléfono*). The main Corfu office of Greece's Telecommunications Organization (OTE) at Mantzárou 3 is open from 6 a.m. to midnight. Here you can send telegrams and dial telephone numbers by yourself or have an operator obtain them for you. Greece's telephone system, among the most advanced in Europe, has direct dialling to many places around the world, including the British Isles and North America. However, international trunk lines are often busy and you may have to wait up to two hours at peak times. Reverse-charge (collect) calls can be made (dial 151 for Europe and 161 for the rest of the world) Monday to Friday.

You can also make a local call or long-distance and international calls from many news-stands and glass phone booths in the capital and around the island. You'll need a stock of 5-, 10- and 20- (sometimes 50-) drachma coins.

To call Corfu Town from an outlying village, use the prefix 0661.

A second telephone and telegraph office, more modern and with more non-Greek signs, is on Kapodistríou, a block behind the Listón. It's open daily from 9 a.m. to 10.30 p.m.

| Telephone Spelling Code | | | | | | | |
|---|---|---|---|---|---|---|---|
| A | Aléxandros | H | Iraklís | N | Nikólaos | T | Timoléon |
| B | Vasílios | Θ | Theódoros | Ξ | Xenofón | Y | Ipsilántis |
| Γ | Geórgios | I | Ioánnis | O | Odisséfs | Φ | Fótios |
| Δ | Dimítrios | K | Konstantínos | Π | Periklís | X | Chrístos |
| E | Eléni | Λ | Leonídas | P | Ródos | Ψ | Psáltis |
| Z | Zoí | M | Menélaos | Σ | Sotírios | Ω | Oméga |

| | |
|---|---|
| Where's the (nearest) post office? | **Pou íne to (kodinótero) tachidromío?** |
| Have you received any mail for …? | **Échete grámmata giá …?** |
| A stamp for this letter/ postcard, please. | **Éna grammatósimo giaftó to grámma/kart postál, parakaló.** |
| express (special delivery) | **exprés** |
| airmail | **aeroporikós** |
| registered | **sistiméno** |
| I want to send a telegram to … | **Thélo na stílo éna tilegráfima sto …** |
| Can you get me this number in …? | **Boríte na mou párete aftó ton arithmó …?** |
| reverse-charge (collect) call | **plirotéo apó to paralípti** |
| person-to-person (personal) call | **prosopikí klísi** |

**COMPLAINTS** (*parápono*). Your hotel manager, the proprietor of the establishment in question or your travel agency representative should be your first recourse for complaints. If you obtain no satisfaction there, Corfu's tourist police (see POLICE) will be extremely interested to hear of anything you feel is wrong. Mentioning your intention to report to the tourist police should get your hotel's swimming pool cleaned, fresh bread served instead of yesterday's and so on.

## C   CONSULATES and EMBASSIES *(proxenío; presvía)*

**British consulate\*:** Alexándras 10, Corfu Town; tel.: 30-055; emergency telephone: 39-211.

**Canadian embassy:** Gennadíou 4, Ipsilántou, 115-21 Athens; tel.: 723-9511.

**U.S. embassy:** Vas. Sofías 91, 115-21 Athens; tel.: 721-2951.

| Where's the British consulate? | **Pou íne to anglikó proxenío?** |
| It's very urgent. | **Íne polí epígon.** |

**CONVERTER CHARTS.** For tire pressure, distance and fluid measures, see page 111. Greece uses the metric system.

**Temperature**

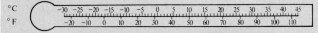

**Length**

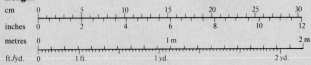

**Weight**

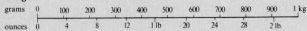

**COURTESIES.** See also MEETING PEOPLE. Corfiotes are friendly, generous, hospitable, and at times elaborately polite—though not in queues! Particularly away from the capital, a glass of water, a cup of coffee or some other welcoming gesture will often greet a tourist. It's meant sincerely and may certainly be accepted in good faith. Practically all Corfiotes shake hands with everybody. It's unheard of for an islander to refuse to help a tourist.

---

\* Also for citizens of Eire and of Commonwealth countries not separately represented.

Greeks, in common with most continental Europeans, wish each
other "bon appetit" before starting a meal. In Greek, the expression is
*kalí órexi!* A common toast when drinking is *stin igiá sas*, meaning
"cheers". A reply to any toast, in the sense of "the same to you" is *epísis*.

**CRIME and THEFT** *(églima; klopí)*. Although it's only common sense
to take precautions such as depositing valuables in your hotel safe,
crime and theft are extremely rare on Corfu.

**CUSTOMS and ENTRY REGULATIONS.** See also DRIVING. Visitors
from EEC (Common Market) countries only need an identity card to
enter Greece. Citizens of most other countries must be in possession of a
valid passport. European and North American residents are not subject to any health requirements. In case of doubt, check with Greek
representatives in your own country before departure.

The following chart shows the quantities of certain major items you
may take into Greece and, upon your return home, into your own
country:

| Into: | Cigarettes | | Cigars | | Tobacco | Spirits | | Wine |
|-------|-----------|----|--------|----|---------|---------|-----|------|
| Greece 1) | 300 | or | 75 | or | 400 g. | 1½ l. | and | 5 l. |
| 2) | 200 | or | 50 | or | 250 g. | 1 l. | or | 2 l. |
| 3) | 400 | or | 100 | or | 500 g. | see 1) | and | 2) |
| Australia | 200 | or | 250 g.or | | 250 g. | 1 l. | or | 1 l. |
| Canada | 200 | and | 50 | and | 900 g. | 1.1 l. | or | 1.1 l. |
| Eire | 200 | or | 50 | or | 250 g. | 1 l. | and | 2 l. |
| N.Zealand | 200 | or | 50 | or | 250 g. | 1.1 l. | and | 4.5 l. |
| S.Africa | 400 | and | 50 | and | 250 g. | 1 l. | and | 2 l. |
| U.K. | 200 | or | 50 | or | 250 g. | 1 l. | and | 2 l. |
| U.S.A. | 200 | and | 100 | and | 4) | 1 l. | or | 1 l. |

1) Residents of Europe, non-duty-free items purchased in EEC countries
   (alcoholic beverage allowances—also for non-European residents)
2) Residents of Europe, items purchased outside EEC countries or in EEC
   countries duty-free (alcoholic beverage allowances—also for non-European
   residents)
3) Residents outside Europe
4) A reasonable quantity

**C** Certain prescription drugs, including tranquillizers and headache preparations, cannot be carried into the country without a prescription or official medical document. Fines—even jail sentences—have been imposed on the unwary tourist.

**Currency restrictions.** Foreign visitors to Greece are not allowed to take into or out of the country more than 3,000 drachmas in local currency. There's no limit on the foreign currency or traveller's cheques you may import or export as a tourist, though amounts in excess of $ 500 or its equivalent must be declared upon arrival.

I've nothing to declare.　　　　　　**Den écho na dilóso típota.**

**D** **DRIVING IN GREECE**

**Entering Greece:** To bring your car into Greece you'll need:

- International Driving Permit
- Car registration papers
- Nationality plate or sticker
- Insurance coverage (the Green Card is no longer obligatory within the EEC, but comprehensive coverage is advisable)

Normally, you're allowed to drive your car in Greece for up to four months. The International Driving Permit (not required for holders of a British licence) can be obtained through your home motoring association.

The standard European red warning triangle is required in Greece for emergencies, as are a fire-extinguisher and a first-aid kit. Seat belts are mandatory. Motorcycle drivers and their passengers should wear crash helmets.

**Driving conditions on Corfu:** Main roads are generally asphalted, but it's folly to drive at high speed. Curves are sometimes not signposted at all, or indicated too late, and they are never banked. When you see a sign to reduce speed, or the warning of a narrowed road, slow down promptly. Secondary roads are sometimes very rough.

Rock slides are common—and dangerous—particularly in the rainy season. Broken shoulders or holes are not unknown on even the best tarred stretches.

Though road signs on main roads and at junctions are in both Greek and Latin letters, on secondary roads and in most villages they tend to be in Greek only.

**Traffic police**—see POLICE

## Fluid measures

imp. gals. 0 ——————— 5 ——————— 10

litres 0 5 10 20 30 40 50

U.S. gals. 0 ——————— 5 ——————— 10

## Tire pressure

| lb./sq. in. | kg/cm² | lb./sq. in. | kg/cm² |
| --- | --- | --- | --- |
| 10 | 0.7 | 26 | 1.8 |
| 12 | 0.8 | 27 | 1.9 |
| 15 | 1.1 | 28 | 2.0 |
| 18 | 1.3 | 30 | 2.1 |
| 20 | 1.4 | 33 | 2.3 |
| 21 | 1.5 | 36 | 2.5 |
| 23 | 1.6 | 38 | 2.7 |
| 24 | 1.7 | 40 | 2.8 |

## Distance

km  0  1  2  3  4  5  6  8  10  12  14  16
miles  0  ½  1  1½  2  3  4  5  6  7  8  9  10

**Road signs:** Most road signs are the standard pictographs used throughout Europe. However, you may encounter the following written signs on Corfu:

| | |
| --- | --- |
| **ΑΔΙΕΞΟΔΟΣ** | No through road |
| **ΑΛΤ** | Stop |
| **ΑΝΩΜΑΛΙΑ ΟΔΟΣΤΡΩΜΑΤΟΣ** | Bad road surface |
| **ΑΠΑΓΟΡΕΥΕΤΑΙ Η ΑΝΑΜΟΝΗ** | No waiting |
| **ΑΠΑΓΟΡΕΥΕΤΑΙ Η ΕΙΣΟΔΟΣ** | No entry |
| **ΑΠΑΓΟΡΕΥΕΤΑΙ Η ΣΤΑΘΜΕΥΣΙΣ** | No parking |
| **ΔΙΑΒΑΣΙΣ ΠΕΖΩΝ** | Pedestrian crossing |
| **ΕΛΑΤΤΩΣΑΤΕ ΤΑΧΥΤΗΤΑΝ** | Reduce speed |
| **ΕΠΙΚΙΝΔΥΝΟΣ ΚΑΤΩΦΕΡΕΙΑ** | Dangerous incline |
| **ΕΡΓΑ ΕΠΙ ΤΗΣ ΟΔΟΥ** | Roadworks in progress (Men working) |
| **ΚΙΝΔΥΝΟΣ** | Caution |

**D**

| ΜΟΝΟΔΡΟΜΟΣ | One-way traffic |
| ΠΑΡΑΚΑΜΠΤΗΡΙΟΣ | Diversion (Detour) |
| ΠΟΔΗΛΑΤΑΙ | Cyclists |
| ΠΟΡΕΙΑ ΥΠΟΧΡΕΩΤΙΚΗ ΔΕΞΙΑ | Keep right |
| ΣΤΑΣΙΣ ΛΕΩΦΟΡΕΙΟΥ | Bus stop |

| (International) Driving Licence | **(diethnís) ádia odigíseos** |
| car registration papers | **ádia kikloforías** |
| Green Card | **asfália aftokinítou** |

| Are we on the right road for ...? | **Ímaste sto sostó drómo giá ...?** |
| Fill the tank, please, top grade. | **Na to gemísete me venzíni soúper, parakaló.** |
| Check the oil/tires/battery. | **Na elénxete ta ládia/ta lásticha/ti bataría.** |
| I've had a breakdown. | **Épatha mía vlávi.** |
| There's been an accident. | **Égine éna distíchima.** |

**E**   **ELECTRIC CURRENT.** The standard current is 220-volt, 50-cycles A.C. Sockets are either two- or three-pin. Larger hotels are often able to supply plug adaptors.

| I need an adaptor/a battery, please. | **Chriázome éna metaschimatistí/mía bataría, parakaló.** |

**EMERGENCIES.** It's unlikely that you'll be anywhere on Corfu where you won't find someone who speaks some English to help in an emergency. But if you're on your own and near a phone, here are some key numbers:

| Police (Corfu Town), all-purpose emergency number | 100 |
| National Tourist Organization | 39-730 |
| Corfu Town hospital, emergencies | 39-403 |
| Fire | 199 |

*Note:* calling Corfu Town from elsewhere on the island (all the above numbers are in the capital), you must first dial the prefix 0661.

Depending on the nature of the emergency, refer also to the separate entries in this section such as CONSULATES AND EMBASSIES, HEALTH AND MEDICAL CARE, POLICE, etc.

Though we hope you'll never need them, here are a few words you **E** may like to learn in advance:

| | | | |
|---|---|---|---|
| Careful | **Prosochí** | Police | **Astinomía** |
| Fire | **Fotiá** | Stop | **Stamatíste** |
| Help | **Voíthia** | | |

**GUIDES and INTERPRETERS\*** *(xenagós; dierminéas)*. Professional, **G** authorized guide-interpreters speaking English, among other languages, work through hotels and travel agencies.

| | |
|---|---|
| We'd like an English-speaking guide. | **Tha thélame éna xenagó na milá i angliká.** |
| I need an English interpreter. | **Chriázome éna ánglo dierminéa.** |

**HAIRDRESSERS** (KOMMΩTHPIO—*kommotírio*) **and BARBERS\*** **H** (KOYPEIO—*kourío*). Prices are, of course, far lower in neighbourhood salons in villages than in the chic hotels. Women should tip the hairdresser about 10% and give a few drachmas to the assistant. For men, tip the barber about 10% and give around 10 drachmas to the *mikró*, the youngster who helps out.

| | |
|---|---|
| I'd like a shampoo and set. | **Thélo loúsimo ke miz-an-plí.** |
| I want a … | **Thélo …** |
| haircut | **koúrema** |
| blow-dry | **chténisma me to pistoláki** |
| permanent wave | **permanád** |
| colour chart | **éna digmatológio** |
| colour rinse | **mía dekolorasión** |
| manicure | **manikioúr** |
| Don't cut it too short. | **Mi ta kópsete kondá.** |
| A little more off (here). | **Lígo pió kondá (edó).** |

**HEALTH and MEDICAL CARE.** Stomach upsets and severe sunburn are the most common tourist complaints, both caused primarily by unwise over-indulgence. Corfu's climate and hygiene standards are fine, and you should be, too—if you take food, drink and sun in moderation.

To be completely at your ease, take out health insurance to cover **113** the risk of illness and accident while on holiday. Your travel agent or insurance company at home will be able to advise you.

Doctors and dentists are concentrated in Corfu Town; your hotel will be able to find you one who speaks English.

The capital's hospital operates a 24-hour emergency clinic which dispatches ambulances (see EMERGENCIES) to any point on the island with admirable speed. Otherwise, call the all-purpose emergency number 100, or the tourist police.

**Pharmacies** (ΦΑΡΜΑΚΕΙΟ—*farmakío*) are easily recognized by the sign outside—a red cross on a white background. One pharmacy is always open in Corfu Town at night and on Sundays—they take it in turns, and your hotel, tour guide or the tourist police will locate the right one.

**Hours:** 8.15 a.m.–1.30 p.m. daily and from 5.15–8.30 p.m. on Tuesdays, Thursdays and Fridays.

Without a prescription, you won't be able to obtain sleeping pills, barbiturates or medicine for stomach upsets. Artificial sweeteners may not be sold to anyone except a diabetic—and you must have a doctor's prescription. For import of prescription drugs to Greece, see under CUSTOMS AND ENTRY REGULATIONS.

| | |
|---|---|
| Where's the nearest (all-night) pharmacy? | **Pou íne to kodinótero (dianikterévon) farmakío?** |
| I need a doctor/dentist. | **Chriázome éna giatró/ odontogiatró.** |

| | |
|---|---|
| an ambulance | **éna asthenofóro** |
| hospital | **nosokomío** |
| sunburn | **éngavma apó ton ílio** |
| sunstroke | **ilíasi** |
| a fever | **piretós** |
| an upset stomach | **varistomachiá** |

**HITCH-HIKING** (*oto-stóp*). Legal on Corfu as everywhere in Greece, hitch-hiking is successfully practised by young and old all over the island.

| | |
|---|---|
| Can you give me/us a lift to …? | **Boríte na me/mas páte méchri to …?** |

**HORSE-CABS** (*ámaxa me álogo*). You'll see several dozen of these handsome 19th-century buggies around Corfu Town, and children of course adore to ride in them. They're also known by the Italian name *carrozza*. Your bargaining skill and the driver's immediate chance of getting other customers should determine the final price, which should always be decided before you set out, and make it absolutely clear that the agreed amount is for your entire little group, *not per person*.

## HOTELS and ACCOMMODATION* (ΞΕΝΟΔΟΧΕΙΟ; ΔΩΜΑΤΙΑ— *xenodochío; domátia*).

As most hotels are fully booked for the high season by package-tour operators abroad, from mid-June until October it may be very, very difficult to find a bed on the island without a reservation. If you do arrive without a reservation, try any travel agency (neither the airport nor the port has a state hotel information service).

The rates on page 101 do not include an optional high-season hike or breakfast. Note that in lower categories, rooms with bath are rare. Price reductions are often offered for children. Ten per cent is added to the bill if you stay only two nights.

Rates and all extra charges (such as hot water if your room has no private facilities) must by law be posted in your hotel room. Offices of the National Tourist Organization of Greece (EOT) maintain a list of all Corfu hotels, their capacities and prices, which you are welcome to study.

Rooms in private homes are rented at usually negotiable rates and conditions. They'll almost always be clean, but you'll rarely have your own shower and toilet.

**Villas:** Corfu has more villas to let than many other tourist centres in Greece. They range from simple cottages, sleeping only two, to lavishly appointed summer homes at monthly rates. If domestic help is not included in the price, personnel can usually be easily found.

In arranging for a villa from abroad, be sure to inquire about accessibility to food shops if you'll be without transport on Corfu.

| | |
|---|---|
| a double/single room | **éna dipló/monó domátio** |
| with/without bath | **me/chorís bánio** |
| What's the rate per night? | **Piá íne i timí giá mía níkta?** |

**LANGUAGE.** See also ALPHABET, and box on page 13. Only in remote spots in the countryside will the non-Greek-speaking tourist have a serious communication problem, but friendly sign language

**L** should help. At least basic English is spoken almost everywhere on Corfu, Italian very often, French fairly frequently, German occasionally.

Here are some Greek expressions to help you along:

| | | | |
|---|---|---|---|
| Good morning | **kaliméra** | Thank you | **efcharistó** |
| Good afternoon | **kalispéra** | Please | **parakaló** |
| Good night | **kaliníkta** | Goodbye | **chérete** |

The Berlitz phrase book GREEK FOR TRAVELLERS covers practically all situations you're likely to encounter in your travels in Greece.

| | |
|---|---|
| Does anybody speak English? | **Milá kanís angliká?** |

**LAUNDRY and DRY-CLEANING** (ΠΛΥΝΤΗΡΙΟ—*plintírio;* ΚΑΘΑ-ΡΙΣΤΗΡΙΟ—*katharistírio*). In this climate it's easy to rinse out small articles yourself. They dry in just a few hours.

During the peak season, allow three or four days for hotel laundry and dry-cleaning services. You'll find it quicker and cheaper to go to the local laundry, but colours may come back faded.

| | |
|---|---|
| Where's the nearest laundry/ dry-cleaners? | **Pou íne to kodinótero plintírio/ katharistírio?** |
| When will it be ready? | **Póte tha íne étimo?** |
| I must have this for tomorrow morning. | **Prépi na íne étimo ávrio to proí.** |

**LOST PROPERTY.** Greeks have a reputation for honesty; Corfu is no exception. If you lose something you have a good chance of getting it back. For anything lost away from your hotel, try the tourist police in Corfu Town (see POLICE).

| | |
|---|---|
| I've lost my wallet/handbag/ passport. | **Échasa to portofóli mou/ti tsánda mou/to diavatirió mou.** |

**M** **MAPS** (*chártis*). There are several island maps; look out for one that makes a clear distinction between dirt tracks and secondary roads, to avoid bumpy rides! Locally produced maps sometimes show roads which are only in the planning stage and occasionally have the names only in Greek letters.

| | |
|---|---|
| a street plan of ... | **éna odikó chárti tou ...** |
| a road map of the island | **éna chárti tou nisioú** |

**MEETING PEOPLE.** Unlike most of Greece, Corfu has a rather "progressive" attitude towards morality—except in its small villages where traditions die hard. Corfiote young ladies accept invitations for drinks or a meal from foreigners, and often seem adroit at circumventing whatever parental discipline there may be in order to enjoy a full social life. But be discreet—this is a small island, and people talk.

Young Corfiote men, perhaps spoiled by the thousands of foreign girls they see each year, can afford to be choosy. Almost never will they persist in pursuing a girl if rebuffed.

## MONEY MATTERS

**Currency.** Greece's monetary unit is the drachma *(drachmí,* abbreviated drs.—in Greek, Δρχ.).

*Coins:* 1, 2, 5, 10, 20 and 50 drachmas.
*Banknotes:* 50, 100, 500, 1,000 and 5,000 drachmas.
For currency restrictions, see CUSTOMS AND ENTRY REGULATIONS.

**Banks and Currency-Exchange Offices** (ΤΡΑΠΕΖΑ: ΣΥΝΑΛΛΑΓΜΑ— *trápeza; sinállagma).* There are banks only in Corfu Town, but several bank buses tour the island, and hotels are also authorized to change money. During high season, the banks are open:

from 8 a.m. to 2 p.m., Monday to Friday.

A few banks in Corfu Town open a couple of hours in the evening and in the morning on the weekend or holidays, but only for currency-exchange operations.

You'll need your passport as identification to change money.

**Credit Cards and Traveller's Cheques** *(pistotikí kárta; "traveller's cheque").* Internationally known credit cards are honoured in most shops (indicated by a sign in the window) and by banks, car hire firms and leading hotels. Most traveller's cheques, in any western currency, are readily accepted as payment or cashed—but take your passport for identification. Eurocheque signs have sprouted around Corfu Town.

**Paying cash.** You may be able to pay for goods in some places with foreign currency, but paying in drachmas is less trouble for everybody.

**Prices.** Shopping around, even in the high tourist season when prices are at predictable peaks, is worthwhile. Patently touristy places charge more than obviously "native" places for everything from a cup of coffee to toothpaste. Certain rates are listed on page 101 to give you an idea of what things cost.

| | |
|---|---|
| I want to change some pounds/dollars. | **Thélo na alláxo merikés líres/meriká dollária.** |
| Do you accept traveller's cheques? | **Pérnete "traveller's cheques"?** |
| Can I pay with this credit card? | **Boró na pliróso me aftí ti pistotikí kárta?** |

**MUSEUM HOURS.** Archaeological Museum and Museum of Asian Art (Corfu Town): 8.30 (Asian Art from 8.45) a.m. to 3 p.m., Monday and Wednesday to Saturday, 9 a.m. to 2 p.m. (Asian Art 9.30 a.m. to 2.30 p.m.) on Sundays, closed on Tuesdays.

**NEWSPAPERS and MAGAZINES** *(efimerída; periodikó).* During the high tourist season British papers, the Paris-based *International Herald Tribune* and some English-language weeklies are on sale in Corfu Town and around the island at tourist centres.

| | |
|---|---|
| Have you any English-language newspapers? | **Échete anglikés efimerídes?** |

**PHOTOGRAPHY** *(fotografía).* A photo shop is advertised by the sign ΦΩΤΟΓΡΑΦΕΙΟ *(fotografío).* There's no Greek-manufactured film.

The greens of Corfu's landscape and the blue-greens of the sea are best photographed in late afternoon when the slanting sun brings out the full depth of the colours (tans also look better then, if you're photographing people). Greeks of all ages love to pose for photographers; to cement a friendship, present a copy of the print to your Corfiote subject.

There are no restrictions on the use of hand-held cameras in Corfu's few small museums, but be prepared to pay a professional's fee for a tripod. For security reasons, it's illegal to use a telephoto lens aboard an aircraft.

| | |
|---|---|
| I'd like some film for this camera. | **Tha íthela éna film giaftí ti michaní.** |
| black-and-white film | **asprómavro film** |
| colour prints | **énchromo film** |
| colour slides | **énchromo film giá sláids** |
| 35-mm film | **éna film triánda pénde milimétr** |
| super-8 | **soúper-októ** |
| How long will it take to develop (and print) this film? | **Se póses iméres boríte na emfanísete (ke na ektipósete) aftó to film?** |
| May I take a picture? | **Boró na páro mía fotografía?** |

**POLICE** *(astinomía).* Corfu has three types of police, and they're all liked and respected by the local populace. The *touristikí astinomía* (tourist police) usually wear light-grey uniforms; aside from helping visitors personally, they accompany state inspectors to hotels and restaurants to ensure that proper standards and prices are maintained. If you have a problem in Corfu Town, see the urban tourist police. The rural tourist police headquarters is also in town, but you'll notice these friendly policemen at various useful places around the island.

The formal rural police or gendarmes are called *chorofílakes.* They wear shoulder cordons with their grey uniforms, and you may see them in white helmets and patrolling on motorcycles.

Finally, Corfu proudly is one of only four places in Greece (with Athens, Piraeus and Patras) to have a separate municipal police force *(astinomía póleon);* its members have some flashy white patrol cars and different uniforms at different seasons: you'll probably see them in light-blue, short-sleeved shirts with grey trousers and caps.

Urban and rural tourist police: Arseníou 35; tel. 39-503

Municipal police: Platía G. Theotóki; tel. 39-509

| | |
|---|---|
| Where's the nearest police station? | **Pou íne to kodinótero astinomikó tmíma?** |

**PUBLIC HOLIDAYS** *(argíes).* Banks, offices and shops are closed on the following national holidays:

**P**

| Jan. 1 | *Protochroniá* | New Year's Day |
|---|---|---|
| Jan. 6 | *ton Theofaníon* | Epiphany |
| March 25 | *Ikostí Pémti Martíou (tou Evangelismoú)* | Greek Independence Day |
| May 1 | *Protomagiá* | May Day |
| Aug. 15 | *Dekapendávgoustos (tis Panagías)* | Assumption Day |
| Oct. 28 | *Ikostí Ogdói Oktovríou* | Óchi ("No") Day, commemorating Greek defiance of Italian ultimatum and invasion of 1940 |
| Dec. 25 | *Christoúgenna* | Christmas Day |
| Dec. 26 | *défteri iméra ton Christougénnon* | St. Stephen's Day |
| Movable dates: | *Katharí Deftéra* | 1st Day of Lent: Clean Monday |
| | *Megáli Paraskeví* | Good Friday |
| | *Deftéra tou Páscha* | Easter Monday |
| | *Análipsis* | Ascension |
| | *tou Agíou Pnévmatos* | Whit Monday ("Holy Spirit") |

*Note:* The dates on which the movable holy days are celebrated often differ from those in Catholic and Protestant countries.

Are you open tomorrow? **Échete aniktá ávrio?**

**R**  **RADIO and TV** *(rádio; tileórasi).* Greek National Radio broadcasts the news in English in the morning, afternoon and evening. On short-wave bands, reception of the World Service of the BBC is extremely clear. Voice of America's English programming is also easily picked up.

Television from Athens in Greek is available on Corfu, with reception depending on the surrounding terrain.

**RELIGIOUS SERVICES** *(litourgía).* The national church is the Greek Orthodox. Visitors of certain other faiths will be able to attend services at the following:

**Catholic:** Ágios Iákovos on Platía Dimarchíou; mass is celebrated several times on Sundays and on weekdays at 8 a.m. from

June to September and at 8.30 a.m. from October to May; on Saturdays from June to October at 7 p.m.

**Anglican:** Holy Trinity Church at Mavíli 21; service in English at 10.30 a.m., Sundays.

**Jewish:** The synagogue is located on Odós Paleológou.

| | |
|---|---|
| Is there a Catholic church/ Protestant church/synagogue near here? | **Ipárchi mía katholikí eklisía/ eklisía diamartiroménon/sinagogí edó kondá?** |
| What time is mass/the service? | **Ti óra archízi i litourgía?** |

**SIESTA.** By 1.30 or 2 p.m. at the latest, Corfu effectively shuts down for its inviolable siesta. People riding motorscooters or playing transistors loudly during siesta time are liable to a fine for disturbing the peace. If you telephone a Corfiote you risk his extreme displeasure. About 5 p.m. when the worst heat is over, people re-emerge, shops reopen, and Corfiotes' favourite time of day begins.

**TAXIS\*** (ΤΑΞΙ—*taxí*). Corfu has about 170 taxis. Drivers are usually familiar with basic English and are honest and friendly. In Corfu Town there are taxi ranks at Kapodistríou, Mantzárou, Spília, Pallas cinema and San Rocco. The central taxi telephone number is 33-811.

What's the fare to …?                **Piá íne i timí giá …?**

**TIME DIFFERENCES.** The chart below shows the time differences in summer between Greece and some selected cities.

| Los Angeles | Chicago | New York | London | **Corfu** |
|---|---|---|---|---|
| 2 a.m. | 4 a.m. | 5 a.m. | 10 a.m. | **noon** |

In winter, Greek clocks are turned back one hour. If your country does the same, the difference in time remains the same as in summer.

What time is it?                **Ti óra íne?**

**TIPPING.** By law, service charges are included in the bill at hotels, restaurants and *tavérnes*. The Greeks aren't tip-crazy, but they do expect you to leave a little more—if the service has been good, of course.

**R**

**S**

**T**

121

**T**    Even if your room or meals are included as part of a package tour, you'll still want to remember the maid and the waiter. The waiter will probably have a *mikró* (an assistant, or busboy), who should get a token of appreciation as well.

| Hotel porter, per bag | 30–50 drs. |
|---|---|
| Maid, per day | 100 drs. |
| Waiter | 5% (optional) |
| Taxi driver | 10% (optional) |
| Tourist guide (½ day) | 100–200 drs. (optional) |
| Hairdresser/Barber | 10% |
| Lavatory attendant | 20 drs. |

**TOILETS** (ΤΟΥΑΛΕΤΤΕΣ—*toualéttes*). In Corfu Town there are public conveniences on Platía G. Theotóki, near the Esplanade bandstand and at the square in the Old Port. In cafés, if you drop in specifically to use the facilities, it's customary to have a coffee or some other drink. Except in modest establishments, there are generally two doors, marked ΓΥΝΑΙΚΩΝ (ladies) and ΑΝΔΡΩΝ (gentlemen).

Where are the toilets?          **Pou íne i toualéttes?**

**TOURIST INFORMATION OFFICES** (*grafío pliroforión tourismoú*). The following branches of the National Tourist Organization of Greece will supply you with a wide range of colourful and informative brochures and maps in English. They will also let you consult the master directory of hotels in Greece, listing all facilities and prices.

**British Isles:** 195-7, Regent St., London WIR 8DL; tel.: (01) 734-5997

**U.S.A.:** 645 5th Ave., New York, NY 10022; tel.: (212) 421-5777;
611 W. 6th St., Los Angeles, CA 90017; tel.: (213) 626-6696;
168 N. Michigan Ave., Chicago, IL 60601; tel.: (312) 782-1084.

**Canada:** 80 Bloor St. West, Suite 1403, Toronto, Ont. M5S 2V1; tel.: (416) 968-2220;
1233 rue de la Montagne, Montreal, Que. H3G 1Z2; tel.: (514) 871-1532.

The main Corfu office of the National Tourist Organization of Greece

**122** *(Ellinikós Organismós Tourismoú*, abbreviated EOT), is located at the capital's prefecture, Diikitírion, a few marble steps from the main post office (tel.: 39-730 or 30-520).

The EOT has a large selection of colour brochures on Corfu and the rest of Greece in several languages, free colour posters advertising Greek points of interest, mimeographed schedules of all buses on Corfu and a list showing the number of beds and room rates at every Corfu hotel.

Where's the tourist office?     **Pou íne to grafío tourismoú?**

**TRAINS.** There are no railways on Corfu. See Buses and Taxis for information on island transport.

**WATER** *(neró).* Corfu's tap water is perfectly safe to drink. A glass of icy (but not ice-)water is normally served with coffee, ice-cream or other café items. Bottled mineral water, usually still rather than fizzy, is also always available (ask for *Loutráki*). And there's that delicious spring-water at Kardáki (see p. 60).

| a bottle of mineral water | **éna boukáli metallikó neró** |
| fizzy (carbonated) | **me anthrakikó** |
| still | **chorís anthrakikó** |

**YACHTING.** Yachts of any nationality coming into Greek waters have set entry and exit points, among which figure Corfu Town. The table below compiled by the Greek Meteorological Service shows average wind velocity (in knots) and direction for the coastal areas that will be of interest to readers of this book.

|  | Ionian Sea Corfu | | Ionian Sea Argostóli | | Ionian Sea Zákinthos | |
|---|---|---|---|---|---|---|
|  | dir. | vel. | dir. | vel. | dir. | vel. |
| April | S.E. | 2.9 | N.W. | 5.8 | N. | 9.8 |
| May | W., S.E. | 2.6 | N.W. | 5.0 | N.E., N. | 9.4 |
| June | W. | 2.9 | N.W. | 5.4 | N.E. | 9.8 |
| July | N.W., W. | 2.9 | N.W. | 5.8 | N. | 10.2 |
| August | N.W. | 2.6 | N.W. | 5.4 | N., N.E. | 9.8 |
| September | S.E. | 2.3 | N.W., N. | 4.4 | N. | 9.0 |
| October | S.E. | 2.6 | N.W., N.E. | 5.0 | N.E. | 10.2 |

**YOUTH HOSTELS** (ΞΕΝΩΝ ΝΕΟΤΗΤΟΣ—*xenón neótitos*). Corfu has one official youth hostel, at Kontokáli, 7 kilometres from Corfu Town, with a total of 30 beds, segregated dormitory style. There's an extra charge if you take a hot shower or have sheets laundered. It's a good idea to inspect the hostel before formally checking in.

## NUMBERS

| | | | |
|---|---|---|---|
| 0 | midén | 18 | dekaoktó |
| 1 | éna | 19 | dekaenniá |
| 2 | dío | 20 | íkosi |
| 3 | tría | 21 | íkosi éna |
| 4 | téssera | 22 | íkosi dío |
| 5 | pénde | 30 | triánda |
| 6 | éxi | 31 | triánda éna |
| 7 | eptá | 40 | saránda |
| 8 | októ | 50 | peninda |
| 9 | enniá | 60 | exínda |
| 10 | déka | 70 | evdomínda |
| 11 | éndeka | 80 | ogdónda |
| 12 | dódeka | 90 | eneninda |
| 13 | dekatría | 100 | ekató |
| 14 | dekatéssera | 101 | ekatón éna |
| 15 | dekapénde | 102 | ekatón dío |
| 16 | dekaéxi | 500 | pendakósia |
| 17 | dekaeptá | 1,000 | chília |

## SOME USEFUL EXPRESSIONS

| | |
|---|---|
| yes/no | **ne/óchi** |
| please/thank you | **parakaló/efcharistó** |
| excuse me/you're welcome | **me sinchoríte/típota** |
| where/when/how | **pou/póte/pos** |
| how long/how far | **póso keró/póso makriá** |
| yesterday/today/tomorrow | **chthes/símera/ávrio** |
| day/week/month/year | **iméra/evdomáda/mínas/ chrónos** |
| left/right | **aristerá/dexiá** |
| up/down | **epáno/káto** |
| good/bad | **kalós/kakós** |
| big/small | **megálos/mikrós** |
| cheap/expensive | **ftinós/akrivós** |
| hot/cold | **zestós/kríos** |
| old/new | **paliós/néos** |
| open/closed | **aniktós/klistós** |
| here/there | **edó/ekí** |
| free (vacant)/occupied | **eléftheri/kratiméni** |
| early/late | **norís/argá** |
| easy/difficult | **éfkolos/dískolos** |
| Does anybody here speak English? | **Milá kanís angliká?** |
| What does this mean? | **Ti siméni aftó?** |
| I don't understand. | **Den katalavéno.** |
| Please write it down. | **Parakaló grápste to.** |
| Is there an admission charge? | **Prépi na pliróso ísodo?** |
| Waiter, please! | **Parakaló!** |
| I'd like … | **Tha íthela …** |
| How much is that? | **Póso káni aftó?** |
| Have you something less expensive? | **Échete káti ftinótero?** |
| What time is it? | **Ti óra íne?** |
| Just a minute. | **Éna leptó.** |
| Help me, please. | **Voithíste me, parakaló.** |

# Index

An asterisk (*) next to a page number indicates a map reference. For index to Practical Information, see inside front cover.

INDEX